Accounting for Sustainable Development Performance

SAM = sustainability assessment model!
[how important]

Accounting for Sustainable Development Performance

Jan Bebbington

AMSTERDAM • BOSTON • HEIDELBERG • LONDON
NEW YORK • OXFORD • PARIS • SAN DIEGO
SAN FRANCISCO • SINGAPORE • SYDNEY • TOKYO

CIMA Publishing is an imprint of Elsevier

PUBLISHING

CIMA Publishing is an imprint of Elsevier
Linacre House, Jordan Hill, Oxford OX2 8DP, UK
30 Corporate Drive, Suite 400, Burlington, MA 01803, USA

First edition 2007

British Library Cataloguing in Publication Data
A catalogue record for this book is available from the British Library

Library of Congress Cataloging-in-Publication Data
A catalog record for this book is available from the Library of Congress

ISBN: 978-0-7506-8559-7

For information on all CIMA Publishing publications visit our
web site at books.elsevier.com

Typeset by Charon Tec Ltd (A Macmillan Company), Chennai, India
www.charontec.com

Transferred to digital printing 2007

07 08 09 10   10 9 8 7 6 5 4 3 2 1

Contents

Preface

The imperative for pursuing sustainable development (SD) is now well recognized and embedded in international, national and regional government processes, including statements of strategic intent from the United Kingdom (UK) Government (most recently in Department for Environment, Food and Rural Affairs, 2005a), in specific policy initiatives (such as the UK emissions trading scheme) as well as within evaluative frameworks (such as strategic environmental assessment). In responding to the ecological and social problems that we currently face, Governments have started the process of shaping and guiding the economic system to deliver SD outcomes rather than a much narrower focus on economic growth. These moves in the political field feed into, and find resonance in, initiatives within the corporate sector that seek to allow organisations to address their social, environment and economic impacts. Indeed, one aspect of the corporate social responsibility agenda addresses how corporations conceive of SD (see, for example, Bebbington and Thomson, 1996), what actions are being undertaken to respond to this agenda and how accounting may transform in response to the need for SD. One particular aspect of this area of practice and research is related to how organisations evaluate the effectiveness of interventions, and indeed to establish a baseline of performance, with respect to whether activities conform to the principles of SD.

While there are numerous avenues along which organisations may travel as they seek to evaluate the extent to which they operate in accordance with the principles of SD, the focus of this piece of work is on project appraisal. The rationale for this focus is that the capital allocation process sets in train a series of decisions that ultimately determine the economic, social and environmental impacts of organisations. Project approval and design, therefore, is a critical linking mechanism between a strategic vision for SD and operational performance. Likewise, the outcomes of corporate activities (reported in stand-alone non-financial reports) will be largely determined by the nature of projects undertaken. For this reason, project appraisal for SD seems an appropriate and valuable focus.

One of the ways in which it is evident that organisations are not operating in a manner consistent with SD is the extent to which negative externalities arise from their operations. Corporations have been described as 'externalising machines' and developments in policy arenas increasingly seek to internalise externalities. Despite this, externalities still arise from economic activity. Full cost accounting describes an approach whereby externalities profiles of organisations as a whole, or for certain activities, are created. It is believed that accounting for externalities will educate organisations about their impacts and organisations will then seek to eliminate them on the basis of this knowledge. This research builds directly on this area of research and practice. In particular, the work describes and evaluates the application of one full cost accounting approach (specifically the Sustainability Assessment Model or SAM) that seeks to quantify the economic, social and environmental impacts of a project, including its externalities profile.

The SAM is a cradle to grave evaluation tool that represents selected economic, resource, environmental and social impacts in monetary terms in the form of a signature graph. While the economic leg of the signature represents money that will eventually flow through the accounts of the organisation, the remainder of the signature represents both positive and negative externalities flowing from the project. This tool was developed and used by BP as they sought to incorporate SD concepts into their operational decisions. This book documents the use of the SAM within BP as well as the reaction to the SAM by a variety of audiences. The research suggests that the SAM is a relatively robust tool in terms of broadly modelling the transformations that arise from a project. More importantly, the SAM has been observed to engage individuals' thinking about SD and this is perhaps its greatest strength.

The wider applicability of the SAM was also considered in the project. Here a number of impediments to widespread adoption of SD modelling were encountered. In particular, the 'fit' between an SD evaluation tool and an organisation's culture, strategy, ethos and existing performance evaluation methods appears to determine the take-up of a SD evaluation tool. For some organisations interviewed the SAM did not mesh with their current evaluation routines and therefore was not seen to be useful. Where the SAM did mesh with the underlying organisational rationalities, however, it was deemed to be an effective way of raising awareness of SD and affecting decision-making processes.

In addition, in expanding the focus from the oil and gas sector to other industries, it was observed that SD performance evaluation tools may need to be different from the SAM to adequately capture the SD issues faced in different sectors. In particular, the political context, regulatory framework, the structure of an industry and the number of different players in a project life cycle are likely to affect the effectiveness of a performance appraisal approach. This suggests that experimentation that is sympathetic to each industry's circumstances needs to be undertaken before any generic tools for SD performance assessment can be developed.

In summary, for organisations to incorporate the demands of SD into their operations some form of performance assessment is necessary but not sufficient. This book, in outlining one approach to SD assessment, demonstrates that SD performance assessment is possible, albeit that such assessment has not been perfected. Looking forward, a number of critical steps in developing accounts of SD performance can be identified. First, organisations should be encouraged to experiment with and developing their own SD evaluation approaches. This is required if organisations are to develop robust linking of aspirations to operational performance. Second, if such experimentation is being undertaken it would be beneficial for such experiments to be disseminated because there is much that organisations can learn from each other. This book demonstrates that SD performance evaluation, as part of investment decision-making processes, is a potentially powerful way to bring SD considerations into the life of organisations. The way in which this may be achieved, however, is dependent on the nature of the organisation involved as well as its industry context.

List of Tables

List of Figures

Acknowledgements

The following people have contributed materially to the success of this research project: Dave Cutteridge (of Inchferry Consulting and formerly sustainable development co-ordinator at BP in Aberdeen), Tom Baxter and Ian Stewart (of Genesis Oil and Gas Consultants), Gordon Harvey and Richard Grant (of BP), interviewees and seminar/workshop participants in the oil and gas, and construction industry. Special thanks also go to BP for funding the development of the SAM in the first place and for enabling continued access to the model for this work. Finally, I would like to thank CIMA for funding this work. Any omissions and errors remain the responsibility of the author.

Bibliographical Material

Jan Bebbington is a Professor of Accounting and Sustainable Development at the University of St Andrews, Scotland and the Director of the St Andrews Sustainability Institute. Contact details: The Gateway, North Haugh, St Andrews, KY16 9SS. Email: jan.bebbington@st-andrews.ac.uk.

Introduction to the Issues

Introduction

The necessity and desirability of pursuing sustainable forms of development have gained considerable currency over the last two decades. Sustainable development (SD) has been championed at inter-governmental, national, regional and sectoral levels (see Table 1.1) and now appears to be cemented in the public policy arena as the only just and appropriate goal for human activities. This move has significant implications for all parts of society as the SD agenda is wide ranging and far reaching (see Bebbington 2001, for a brief history of the development of the concept of SD within a business and accounting context). While the SD agenda affects us all as individuals (in the context of being consumers and as citizens) it also affects the context within which we undertake our professional duties: hence the focus of this book is on accounting for SD performance.

Whilst there are considerable problems with defining SD, Jacobs (1991, p. 60) argues that there is stable ground which emerges from the plethora of literature in the area and suggests that there are three core aspects of SD: (1) the need to embed environmental considerations in the economic policy-making process; (2) the inescapable commitment to equity both between and within generations (Tisdell, 1993, notes that the ethical basis for this is Rawls's (1972) principle of justice) and (3) a reconsideration of the meaning of development which recognises the concept as being wider than growth (see, for example, Yanarella and Levine, 1992; Norgaard, 1988; Redclift, 1987). Added to this is a conceptualisation of SD as being an ongoing process which moves activities away from unsustainability. Thus the definition of sustainability (as the endpoint) and SD (as the process) removes the need to specify all the intermediate conditions and requirements for a sustainable world. Pirages (1994) adopts this approach while noting that since 'the core problem of the sustainability problematique is a mutual adjustment of the sociocultural genome and the physical environment, there can be no such permanent solutions and fixed definitions of sustainability' (p. 200). Rather, the focus is on the presence of unsustainable states and an iterative process of social, economic and environmental adjustment which will remove the unsustainable elements. While this approach does not lead to a tight specification of all the elements which could be seen as constituting SD, a 'vague definition is better than spurious precision and

Table 1.1: Examples of SD imperatives at inter-governmental, national and regional levels

Inter-governmental

◆ The 1972 United Nations Conference on the Human Environment (in Stockholm) was the first world conference to address what became the SD agenda. At this conference the term 'eco-development' was proposed to describe the process of ecologically sound development with positive management of the environment for human benefit (Holdgate et al., 1982, p. 7; McCormick, 1986, p. 182). At the same time it was stated that 'environment management had as its broad objective the development of comprehensive planning and the protection and enhancement of the environment for future generations' (Holdgate et al., 1982, p. 10).

◆ The foreward of the World Conservations Strategy notes:
'[h]uman beings, in their quest for economic development and enjoyment of the riches of nature, must come to terms with the reality of resource limitation and the carrying capacities of ecosystems, and must take account of the needs of future generations. This is the message of conservation. For if the object of development is to provide for social and economic welfare, the object of conservation is to ensure Earth's capacity to sustain development and to support life' (IUCN, 1980, p. I).

◆ The Brundtland Report reinforced the need for SD which was seen as having the potential to build a prosperous, just and secure future (United Nations World Commission on Environment and Development, 1987, p. 1, hereafter UNWCED) and provides the commonly accepted definition of SD as being development which 'meets the needs of the present without compromising the ability of future generations to meet their own needs' (UNWCED, 1987, p. 8).

◆ The World Bank (1995) notes that a 'quiet revolution has been under way during the first half of the 1990s, as environmental sustainability has become a theme of policy making around the world' (p. 2) and suggested that Rio captured 'the growing consensus and dramatically accelerating the momentum for change' (World Bank, 1995, p. 2).

◆ The United Nations Conference on Environment and Development (Rio Earth Summit in 1992) produced a 27 principle Rio Declaration on Environment and Development including:
  – Human beings are at the centre of concerns for SD. They are entitled to a healthy and productive life in harmony with nature (principle 1).
  – The right to development must be fulfilled so as to equitably meet developmental and environmental needs of present and future generations (principle 3).
  – In order to achieve SD, environmental protection shall constitute an integral part of the development process and cannot be considered in isolation from it (principle 4). See also www.un.org/geninfo/bp/enviro.html.

◆ Ten years after the Rio Earth Summit the United Nations held a World Summit on Sustainable Development in Johannesburg. This led to a further reaffirmation of the role of SD by 'the representatives of the peoples of the world ... We commit ourselves to building a human, equitable and caring global society, cognizant of the need for human dignity for all ... children of the world ... challenged all of us to ensure that through our actions they will inherit a world free of the indignity and indecency occasioned by poverty, environmental degradation and patterns of unsustainable development ... we assume a collective responsibility to advance and

(continued)

strengthen the interdependent and mutually reinforcing pillars of SD – economic development, social development and environmental protection – at the local, national, regional and global levels' (drawn from the Johannesburg Declaration on Sustainable Development. See also www.johannesburgsummit.org).

National

◆ In March 2005 the UK Government refreshed the UK SD strategy, first developed in 1999, to provide a shared framework for SD (Department for Environment, Food and Rural Affairs, 2005a). Under this umbrella framework the various elements of devolved government also developed their own strategies and implementation plans for these strategies. The framework agreement, however, provides the context for these regional strategies. Two key outcomes are sought from an SD strategy:
  – Living within environmental limits (Respecting the limits of the planet's environment, resources and biodiversity – to improve our environment and ensure that the natural resources needed for life are unimpaired and remain so for future generations.)
  – Ensuring a strong, healthy and just society (Meeting the diverse needs of all people in existing and future communities, promoting personal wellbeing, social cohesion and inclusion, and creating equal opportunity for all.)

These are to be achieved via:
  – Achieving a sustainable economy (Building a strong, stable and sustainable economy which provides prosperity and opportunities for all, and in which environmental and social costs fall on those who impose them (polluter pays), and efficient resource use is incentivised.)
  – Promoting good governance (Actively promoting effective, participative systems of governance in all levels of society – engaging people's creativity, energy and diversity.)
  – Using sound science responsibly (Ensuring policy is developed and implemented on the basis of strong scientific evidence, whilst taking into account scientific uncertainty (through the Precautionary Principle) as well as public attitudes and values.)

The shared priorities for immediate action within the UK are:
  – Sustainable consumption and production.
  – Climate change and energy.
  – Natural resource protection and environmental enhancement.
  – Sustainable communities.
See also www.sustainable-development.gov.uk/index.htm.

Regional

◆ The Scottish Executive (2002) states that the 'fundamental aim of SD is to secure the future. We have seen how actions in the past have made life more difficult for us today. Developing sustainably means ensuring that our actions today do not limit our quality of life in the future. So our vision is based on the principles that we should:
  – Have regard for others who do not have access to the same level of resources and the wealth generated.

(continued)

Table 1.1: (continued)

   – Minimise the impact of our actions on future generations by radically reducing our use of resources and by minimising environmental impacts.
   – Live within the capacity of the planet to sustain our activities to the replenish resources which we use' (p. 2). See also www.sustainable.scotland.gov.uk.
♦ The Government of Wales Act (1998) requires, under section 121, that the Welsh Assembly makes a scheme for SD in Wales. SD is described as adopting principles that 'mean address[ing] social, economic and environmental issues at the same time when and planning for long-term benefits' (Welsh Assembly Government web site). In addition, the First Minister for Wales, Rhordri Morgan, states that 'SD is not an option that will go away – it is the only way forward' (Welsh Assembly Government, 2004, p. i). See www.wales.gov.uk/themessustainabledev.

much better than ignoring the issue' (Tisdell, 1988, p. 382) and it is likely that the concept will remain 'fuzzy, elusive, contestable and/or ideologically controversial for some time to come' (Gladwin et al., 1995, p. 3).

The elements of the SD agenda, and especially the need to embed environmental and social elements into decision making, have begun to affect the language used by companies who are increasingly asserting that they seek to act in accordance with the principles of SD. One way in which a commitment to SD is evidenced is by the production of social, environmental, SD and/or corporate social responsibility reports by organisations (see, for example, the Global Reporting Initiative guidelines which purports to set a framework for SD reporting (www.globalreporting.org)). For a web based resource of stand-alone reports from around the world see the Corporate Register (http://www.corporateregister.com/). While external reporting purportedly provides a representation to the outside world of a firm's achievements with regard to SD, what is less clear is whether or not, and if so to what extent, SD plays a role in guiding organisational activities. If organisations are seeking to report on their contribution to SD, one may expect that there are some internal mechanisms which guide their activities towards this goal. For example, one might imagine that SD is incorporated within strategic and other planning process, in policy decisions, capital allocation routines and in performance evaluation. As these processes are not directly visible to those outside of the organisation, there is less information in the public domain about how organisations are internally addressing SD (see, for example,

Bennett and James, 1998a, b; Ditz et al., 1995; Gray and Bebbington, 2001; Schaltegger, 1996; Schaltegger and Burritt, 2000).

This work focuses on these internal decision-making processes and, in particular, on capital allocation processes and how they may incorporate demands for SD performance. The rational for this focus is twofold. In the first instance, capital allocation processes and routines are the channels through which strategies and planning for SD could meaningfully be implemented. Second, if one wishes to affect operational performance (with a focus on improving SD performance) then considering issues at the planning phase of those activities provides considerable scope for affecting outcomes. If one can find evidence of SD being incorporated into capital allocation processes then *prima facie* one could have more faith in organisations' assertions that they are seeking to work towards SD goals.

In addition, a focus on modelling SD impacts of corporate decisions via some project evaluation process is in keeping with the development of a separate but related theme in the SD literature, that of accounting for externalities. Bebbington et al. (2001) provide an extensive review of full cost accounting covering: the impetus for the development of this accounting tool, the principles of full cost accounting, a review of full cost accounting experiments which are in the public domain and evidence of business and accountants' views of full cost accounting. They conclude that full cost accounting provides a potential way to incorporate SD principles into corporate decision-making and may also enable 'society to better understand the linkages between economic activity and the pursuit of SD' (Bebbington et al., 2001, p. 136). Further, they quote Popoff and Buzzelli (1993) who suggest that 'when implemented correctly, full cost accounting will improve environmental performance more than any other action, program or regulation in play today' (p. 7) and further, that full cost accounting 'may well be the most important step down the path to SD' (p. 8).

In brief (but see also Chapter 2), full cost accounting involves developing accounting tools so that 'the consumption and use of environmental [for example] resources are accounted for as part of the full cost of production and reflected in market prices' (European Commission, 1992, Vol. II, p. 67, hereafter EC). The aim of such an approach is to ensure that externalities of activities are identified and accounted for. Externalities are described as arising where 'the social or economic activities of one group of persons have an impact on another group and when that impact is not fully accounted for by the first group' (EC, 1995, Vol. II, p. 413). Negative externalities are generally those things that register as being 'problems' in the political sphere (for example, greenhouse gas emissions, air pollution and exploitation of workers) and which demonstrate that current economic activity is not in accordance with the principles of SD. Accounting for externalities in the form of full cost accounting, therefore, is a central plank in the development of accounts of SD performance.

As a result, we have a situation where there is recognition that there is a need to incorporate SD principles into internal decision making with full cost accounting being proposed as a way to do this. What is more, there are several publicly reported attempts to undertake full cost accounting which can be drawn on in order to understand the efficacy of this accounting technique. Further, and subsequent to Bebbington et al.'s (2001) research report, another full cost accounting model has been developed which explicitly focuses on SD (the majority of full cost accounting experiments undertaken before 2001 focused exclusively on environmental externalities and as such they were examples of environmental accounting, but not of themselves complete accounts of SD performance), but see Bent (2004) for a more recent account of social externalities.

In particular, Baxter et al. (2004) report upon the creation of a capital allocation model developed and used by BP in order to insert the SD rationale into project decision making. This book takes the Sustainability Assessment Model (SAM) as the starting point of a broader investigation of both the efficacy of this particular accounting tool as well as the possibilities for other approaches to incorporating SD into decision-making processes within a variety of organisations. The work, therefore, extends and develops the full cost accounting theme developed by Bebbington et al. (2001) to examine one possible model in much greater depth and within the context of organisational decision making.

Outline of research undertaken

The work undertaken comprises three distinct elements. The first element introduces a context for thinking about accounting for SD performance and proposes the SAM as one way of achieving this outcome. This element of the work also provides an in-depth examination of BP's experience with the SAM. The second element of the research extends its focus to the oil and gas industry more generally to uncover how other organisations operationalise SD in their decision making. Further, views of the likely usefulness of the SAM have been elicited from within this industry. The final element extends the industry focus of the work to examine (in less detail than the analysis within the oil and gas industry) how the construction and electricity generation industries are starting to think about accounting for SD performance. Each element of the work is introduced in more detail below.

The first element of the study examines the SAM itself. It traces the development of the SAM and describes how it seeks to model SD in the project evaluation/capital allocation process within BP. The SAM has been developed for several different sorts of projects within BP and SAM signatures produced by each project are presented. In addition, how individuals within BP view the SAM and how it has been viewed by project teams who have sought to use it to inform their decision-making processes are considered. This element of the book is designed to create an in-depth picture of this particular accounting tool and its application in concrete organisational settings.

The second element of the study involves gathering a broader set of perceptions about the possibilities for project appraisal for SD from within the oil and gas industry. In particular, interviews were conducted with people in the industry who have SD responsibilities and these interviews explored aspects of project management and performance assessment as well as how organisations have sought to evaluate their SD performance more generally. In addition, a conference which examined the theme of 'measuring, managing and target setting for SD' was undertaken as part of this project and feedback from participant workshops have been incorporated into the book. The purpose of this element of the study is twofold. In the first instance, a broader understanding of how SD is incorporated into operations within one industry is developed. Second, the various ways in which project evaluation has and could be undertaken is drawn together along with a formal evaluation of the SAM approach.

The third and final part of the study sought to explore, in a less detailed manner, the possibilities for SD evaluation within two other industries. The industries in which this investigation focused were the construction and electricity generation industries. These industries were chosen as comparators for the study because they have been more visibly proactive in thinking about SD (for example, construction has industry-wide SD strategies), their activities focus on particular production sites (and hence mirror the project focus of the oil and gas industry) and they have a choice of more/less sustainable technologies for, respectively, creating the built environment and generating energy. This part of the project involved interviews with relevant industry participants as well as a workshop on measuring, managing and target setting for SD with the construction industry. The outcomes of this investigation provide a context within which to gain a broader picture of how SD elements could be incorporated into organisational evaluations and the possible applicability of the SAM to other industry settings.

The structure of the book

The book follows the elements which are outlined above. This chapter constitutes the introduction to the study as well as providing an overview of SD.

Chapter 2 describes the principles behind developing tools for measuring, managing and target setting for SD. There are three broad approaches which appear to be used in this area: (1) indicators for SD, (2) indicators for SD with some evaluation rule applied to the indicators and (3) models for evaluating SD performance which use a common metric (often, but not exclusively, money). Examples of each of these approaches are provided.

Chapter 3 focuses on the SAM as a particular example of a monetised model for SD evaluation. The method used to construct the SAM is described and work undertaken to 'sense check' the SAM is reported on. This chapter starts the process of evaluating the efficacy of the SAM in doing what it purports to do.

Chapter 4 extends the discussion to the application of the SAM within BP's project appraisal/capital allocation process. Particular case studies of the application of the SAM are presented along with internal organisational participants perceptions of the SAM and its use within the organisation. In addition, the SAM strengths and weaknesses, as perceived by industry participants and commentators, are reported on.

Chapter 5 broadens out discussion to the use of appraisal techniques for SD within the oil and gas industry and reports on the various approaches that other organisations use or consider useful for SD evaluation.

Chapter 6 continues the theme from Chapter 5 but explores the applicability of the SAM to two other industries, namely construction and electricity generation. A series of interviews with industry participants are reported on, as is a workshop with representatives of the construction industry.

Chapter 7 draws the study together with a discussion of the possibilities for measuring, managing and target setting for SD. The possibilities of tools, such as the SAM, effectively incorporating SD into internal decision making are the primary focus of this chapter.

Tools for Measuring, Managing and Target Setting for Sustainable Development

Introduction

As is evident from Chapter 1, sustainable development (SD) is a difficult concept to define with precision and this makes evaluating SD performance challenging. Most SD commentators, however, agree that SD is comprised of three elements: economic, social and environmental aspects. It is usual to conceptualise the interactions between these elements thus: that current economic activity leads to social and environmental outcomes which are often neither ecologically sustainable (that is, within the carrying capacity of the planet or local environments) nor socially just (that is, needs of all people alive today are not met and by definition, neither of the needs of future generations). SD is thus a form of economic activity (leading to development) that meets the dual criteria of ecological and social sustainability.

Figure 2.1 demonstrates the two main ways SD is conceptualised. The first diagram is the most common way in which SD is represented with SD arising from the intersection of the three elements. Alternatively, SD is conceptualised (*inter alia*, by the Forum for the Future) as a series of concentric rings in which the natural environment provides the physical basis from which society is sustained which in turn is expressed, in part, by the economic world. Clearly the mental picture which one has of SD will affect what tools one believes will help you measure SD.

Attempting to provide an account of the SD profile of a set of interactions most usually focuses on the three elements of SD (Elkington's, 1997, 'triple bottom line'). Approaches in the open literature that attempt to measure SD usually take one of the three forms. The first utilises a variety of indicators, each of which relates to some aspect of SD. Under this approach indicators are presented together and are seen to provide an overview of SD performance. The particular way in which the indicators combine to provide on overview is, however, not formally articulated under this approach. Rather, individuals are left to combine the indicators as they see fit.

The second approach to SD evaluation uses indicators but combines these with some explicit decision rule with regard to whether or not SD is being achieved. Under this approach there is the possibility of a single figure being drawn out which purports to represent the overall performance of the system under evaluation.

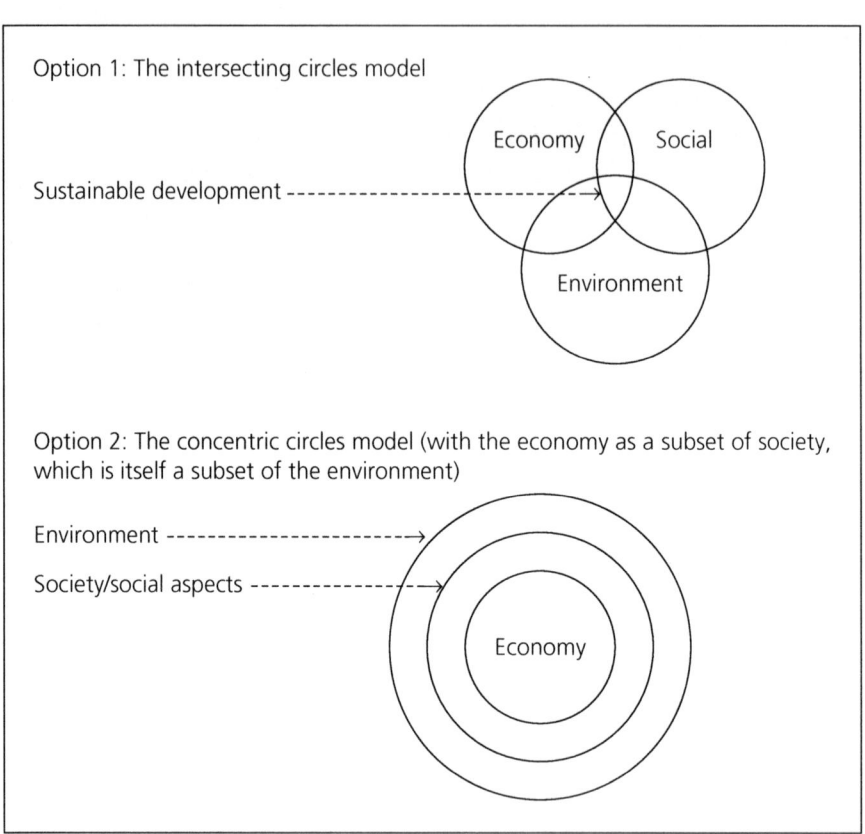

Figure 2.1 Conceptualising SD.

The third and final approach is one which creates an account of SD performance using a common metric. Often that metric is money, but it need not be. This final approach includes full cost accounting (FCA) as an approach to articulating SD and this technique is the focus of this work. In contrast to the other approaches which either implicitly or explicitly combine the various elements of SD together, monetised approaches weight and combine elements of SD through the method of monetisation. As a result, the values implicit in the approach may not be as obvious as in the second approach. Each approach, with examples, will be subject to more in-depth discussion below.

Indicators for SD

At its simplest, SD accounting involves listing indicators that purport to describe aspects of a system's performance that relate to SD.

Indicator lists may comprise any number of items. For example, an indicator may reflect that some feature is present (an environmental management system certified against some standard approach). This type of indicator has a bi-modal characteristic (either the characteristic is present or not). Other indicators may be metrics of a quantitative (including financial) nature where quantities of pollutants produced in a certain time frame or from a particular source are listed. Likewise, money spent to remedy environmental impacts or costs borne by other members of society due to externalities may be calculated. Externalities may be both positive and negative (although negative externalities tend to be more prevalent and of greater concern to policy makers). Likewise, externalities may be of any type: economic, social or environmental.

Table 2.1 provides an example of indicators for SD (without formal weighting) drawn from the Scottish Executive. Most national and devolved governments have similar types of indicator projects of varying degrees of complexity.

Table 2.1 illustrates a number of points which are common to indicator sets of this type. The indicators are gathered under four headings which reflect both environmental and social factors, and thus cover these two elements of SD. The economic leg of the 'triple bottom line' is not directly addressed as a separate element in this context (although it appears in the form of gross domestic product (GDP) in two of the indicators). Rather, the economic system will dictate the types of outcomes which emerge in the categories listed. For example, waste production is, *inter alia*, a function of the costs of various waste disposal alternatives, the taxation system and the market for recovered/recycled materials. While the nature of the economic system is not explicitly outlined in an indicator set, it is implicit in the elements described.

Further, it is apparent from the list that the indicators measure quite different aspects of the SD problem set. For example, air pollution is not measured in physical terms but in terms of the number of locations at which air quality requires monitoring. The implication is that the fewer air management areas an economy has the more sustainable it is. In addition, some of the indicators are total impact/activity (for example, total road travel or total greenhouse gas emissions) while others measure the capacity of the system to

Table 2.1: Indicators for SD in Scotland

Resource use

1. Sustainable prosperity (index of CO_2 emission divided by GDP)
2. Work: people as a resource (percentage of unemployed working age people)
3. Population structure (proportion of population which is working age)
4. Waste: production (municipal waste arisings)
5. Waste: recycling (percentage of total household waste recycled)
6. Waste: land-filled (biodegradable municipal wastes land-filled)
7. Climate change (greenhouse gas carbon equivalent emissions)
8. Air quality (number of air quality management areas)
9. Water quality (kilometres identified as poor or seriously polluted)
10. Biodiversity (percentage of Biodiversity Action Plan species and habitats which are identified as stable or increasing)
11. Sea fisheries (proportion of fish stocks which are within safe biological limits)

Energy

12. Energy: consumed (in gigawatt hours)
13. Energy: renewable (percentage from renewable sources)

Travel

14. Travel: distance (total vehicle kilometres)
15. Travel: industry (freight intensity as measured by tonne kilometres moved and GDP)
16. Travel: mode (percentage of journeys to work not using a car)
17. Travel: accessibility (percentage of households within 6 minutes walk of a bus service)

Social justice

18. Home life (percentage of children living in workless households)
19. Preparing for life (percentage of 16–19 year olds who are not in education, training or employment)
20. Fuel poverty (total number of people living in fuel poverty)
21. Social concern (number of homeless people entitled to permanent accommodation)
22. Crime (total number of crimes)
23. Volunteering (percentage of people taking part in voluntary activities)
24. Health (life expectancy at birth)

Source: Scottish Executive (2002).

create an outcome which would be preferred (for example, accessibility of bus transport is a pre-condition to people being able to use it). Other indicators are composite in nature (items 1 and 15 in Table 2.1) where performance in one element is linked to changes in another.

All indicator sets have inherent strengths and weaknesses, regardless of how well they have been developed. A significant weakness is that indicators are most usually simplifications of the system under consideration (see Bell and Morse, 1999 for more details) and as such may not only fail to describe the system under scrutiny but, by providing poor information, will lead to actions which do not achieve the outcomes sought. This is almost certainly likely to be the case when one is attempting to describe something as complex and interrelated as the SD performance of a country or economy. One formal and systematic approach to trying to remedy this problem can be found in a framework within which indicators can be set which has been developed by the European Environmental Agency (EEA).

The EEA categorises indicators according to how they link to drivers, pressures, states, impacts and responses to environmental and other concerns (the DPSIR framework). This DPSIR framework is designed to enable decision/policy makers to use indicators more effectively. By way of example, Table 2.2 outlines a sample of the indicators used by the EEA in the area of managing transport impacts using the DPSIR framework. As is evident from the table the various indicators are linked to each other but each deals with a different aspect of the issue under consideration (in this instance seeking to stabilise road transport volumes). The indicators are measures of aspects of the issues under consideration with each stage feeding to the next. For example, an action under the responses section will feed into aspects of drivers, drivers create pressures which lead to states and so on. In this way, indicators are linked into a chain of causality which could plausibly lead to changes in SD performance.

In summary, one approach to dealing with SD performance evaluation is to make and report upon measures of aspects of SD in the form of indicators. Indicators can take many forms and, in reality, will depend both on the availability of data as well as a belief on behalf of those who develop them on an ability to affect the indicator of choice. This latter point goes some way to explaining why, for example, the Scottish Executive indicators in Table 2.2 focuses on household and municipal wastes as these are waste arisings that the Executive has the ability to control. In addition, indicators ideally should not be 'innocent', in that a change in the indicator should indicate if the system in question is performing better or worse in

Table 2.2: DPSIR approach to transport indicators

Category of indicators	Example of indicators (see http://themes.eea.eu.int/indicators, for more information on all indicators used)
Drivers	◆ Freight transport demand ◆ Access to public transport
Pressures	◆ Oil pollution incidents arising from transport (for example, oil discharges from ships at sea) ◆ Greenhouse gas emissions from transport
States	◆ CO_2 concentrations in atmosphere ◆ Degree of fragmentation of ecosystems due to roads
Impacts	◆ Percentage of the population exposed to air pollution which is in excess of EU air quality standards
Responses	◆ Road pricing measures adopted ◆ Development of transport strategies ◆ Differential transport taxes on the basis of environmental externalities from different modes of transport

relation to the goal of SD. Likewise, the reasons for changes in indicators, where possible, should be evident, which is one reason why complex indicators are often avoided. Lists of indicators, however, do not necessarily provide evidence on whether or not, as a whole, a system is becoming more or less sustainable. In order to make such a judgement, some form of assessment on the basis of indicators may be needed.

Indicators for SD with formal assessment criteria

It was noted above that a weakness of indicator sets is that while each indicator may be of interest to a reader, how a set of indicators can be understood to indicate progress towards or away from SD is not obvious. As a result, indicator sets are sometimes coupled with explicit decision rules or weightings which provide a composite picture of SD performance. Three examples are provided of indicators with assessment methods, the first one relates to a country-wide evaluation of aspects which are intimately related to SD. This method is the Human Development Index (HDI) which uses indicators and formal assessment criteria to evaluate a country's development performance. The other examples (found in Tables 2.3 and 2.4) are more micro level evaluations at the corporate and project level of resolution, respectively, which again could be seen to be linked to SD aspects. Indicators which have SD relevance, in these latter examples, are combined with explicit decision-making rules that weight those indicators that are believed to matter the most in pursuing SD.

There are several approaches to measuring the performance of economies that are broader than the traditional GDP-driven measure of welfare. These alternative approaches are akin to an SD evaluation. Two of these use economic numbers as the base (and hence are considered in the next section). The HDI, however, is of the nature of an indicator set with weightings designed to provide an indicator of a key element of SD, the performance of a country in human development terms.

The HDI is a composite index that seeks to measure the average achievement in a country in three basic dimensions of human development: (1) a long healthy life (measured by life expectancy at birth); (2) knowledge (measured by the adult literacy rate and the combine gross enrolment ratio for primary, secondary and tertiary schools) and (3) a decent standard of living (measured by GDP per capita purchasing power parity US dollars: that is, the differences in national price levels are eliminated from the analysis). These elements result in three indexes being calculated for each country (based on life expectancy, education and GDP) and the resulting HDI is an average of these indexes. Each year a list of highest to lowest performing countries are published with historical trends providing a glimpse of when and how countries move in this ranking (see United Nations Development Programme, 2004, pp. 127–142, see also www.nationmaster.com which has the HDI and numerous other statistics by country).

In moving to a sub-national level of analysis, there are a huge variety of approaches to using indicators with assessment. Two examples are provided here at the entity and the project level of assessment focusing on SD.

The first (in Figure 2.2) relates to Risk and Policy Analysts (RPA) who are a small consultancy firm in the UK providing services in the area of risk management and decision techniques. RPA produced sustainability reports in 2001 and 2002 (no reports appear to have been produced since that time), and in 2002 they developed a way

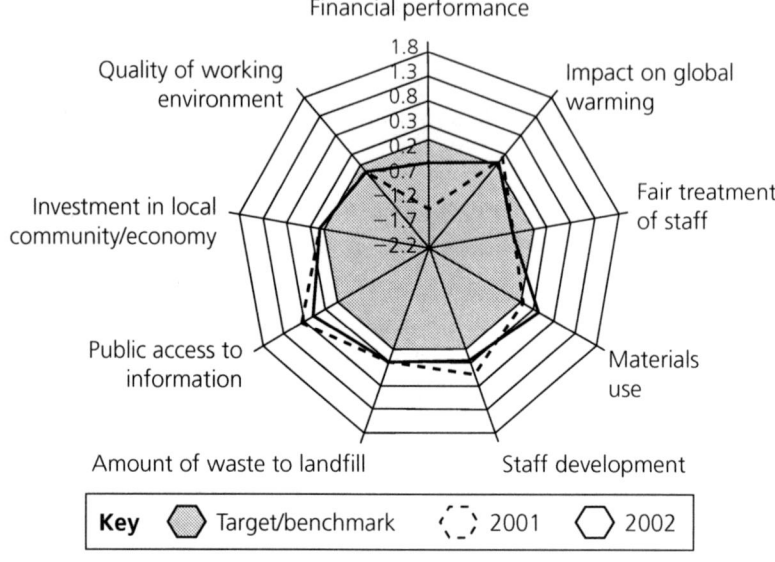

Figure 2.2 RPA sustainability performance.
Source: Risk and Policy Analysts (2002) p. 8, see also www.rpaltd.co.uk.

of mapping their overall SD performance along a series of indicator categories. These categories included financial performance, impact on global warming and fair treatment of staff, as evident from the ends of the lines in Figure 2.2. These indicator categories have been ranked by RPA's stakeholders as being the most to the least important (with financial performance being ranked as being most important and with the level of importance falling as you move clockwise around the map of indicators): quality of working environment, for example, is the least important performance category, as ranked by stakeholders. These elements then provide the basis for an evaluation of SD performance.

Rather than reporting on absolute performance, the organisation sought to provide an indication of how their performance relates to targets/benchmarks that, if reached, would be deemed to be progressing towards SD. Benchmarks for performance were taken from a variety of sources and they provide the following information for how targets and performance have been translated into performance reporting in Figure 2.2.

33.8t of CO_2 was emitted in this (2002) reporting period. In the last reporting period we identified a target of 32.4t CO_2 (to be achieved by 2010 under the UK commitment to the Kyoto Protocol). We are currently over target by a factor of 0.04 calculated by dividing the difference over/under the target value (33.8−32.4 = 1.4) by the target value (32.4). Of course, there are also occasions when we are within the target. For example, our actual labour turnover is 10% and our target is 20%. In this case, the score is expressed as a negative value to denote the fact that we have gone beyond the target: we are under the target by a factor of −0.5 in the case of labour turnover (i.e. we are performing twice as well as we 'have to') (RPA, 2002, p. 7).

As a result, the picture of performance contained in Figure 2.2 provides an indication of the dimensions of performance which the stakeholders in this organisation deemed to be important along with a measure of performance along that dimension relative to a benchmark of SD performance (itself informed by 'official' measures of what would constitute an adequate SD performance standard). In this manner disparate indicators have been presented on one spatial domain. Further, it is assumed that this technique will provide an overall indication of the extent to which this organisation has demonstrated performance which is consistent with an SD benchmark.

The second example of micro level assessments of SD involves Infrastructure Auckland (IA): a public body in New Zealand who existed from 1998 until 2004. IA was created in order to allocate funds for infrastructure development in New Zealand's largest city, Auckland. Auckland had and has 'classic' problems of urban sprawl (that is, relatively low density living, a car culture and a geography which dictates long, thin patterns of development). Local authorities in the area believed that unless effective transport corridors were developed and storm water issues were dealt with, the development of Auckland would be hampered. IA was vested with a number of assets with organisations bidding for funding to undertake infrastructure projects around transport and storm water. A key part of the bidding process was the use of a multi-criteria analysis to evaluate project benefits under the headings of economic, environmental and social outcomes. Thus, although IA did not formally use the language of SD in their evaluation, in effect their project evaluation approach operationalised the 'triple bottom line'.

The approach to SD evaluation was to establish categories (see Table 2.3) which were deemed to be important for the decision under consideration. Under each category a scoring system for performance

Table 2.3: IA multiple criteria analysis: criteria and weightings

Criteria	Weighting
Transport model scoring system	
Access to/around region	9.8
Commuting time savings	9.8
Quality of travelling experience	9.2
Work and freight travel time savings	7.8
Development of social infrastructure	7
Air quality outcomes	6.6
Project efficiency	6.2
Regional economic growth	6.2
Community identity and belonging	5.8
Noise outcomes	5.3
Vehicle operating cost savings	5.1
Water quality outcomes	4.5
Visual and landscape outcomes	4.4
Sense of safety	4.4
Transport safety	4.2
Awareness of conservation	3.6
Storm water model scoring system	
Water quality outcomes	50
Public health consequences of water based recreation	8
Regional economic growth	6
Visual and landscape outcomes	6
Community identity and belonging	6
Awareness of conservation	6
Opportunities for water based recreation	6
Opportunities for land based recreation	4
Project efficiency	4
Sense of safety	4

Source: Primary source documents from IA (scoring system for all projects submitted beginning January 2003).

was created (ranging from 1 to 5). For some categories the score is determined by the extent to which outcomes fit within predefined numerical categories (for example, quantitative measures of water quality). In other categories the score is determined by matching qualitative descriptions of performance to the 1–5 scale. In this way both 'soft' and 'hard' data have been converted into a basis which enables comparison. The scores assigned in each area are then weighted according to the importance of each element in the overall assessment of project performance with a total score emerging from this process.

The use of the IA approach had two outcomes. First, the process of filling in questionnaires and providing data (to support the process of assigning grades to each category in the assessment) appeared to engage applicants' thinking around the issues IA wished to have addressed. In addition, IA was able to 'drill down' through projects to establish what particular elements drove the final score and to develop performance improvements in that area. Having noted this, the final score depends entirely on the robustness of the method taken. In the area of SD evaluation the first thing that one can hope for in this context is that there is transparency around the scoring and weighting process. Second, if an evaluation approach is consistently applied a ranking of projects from best to worst can be useful, regardless of the finer detail of the evaluation approach. IA, during its lifetime, appeared to satisfy both of these criteria.

All of the approaches outlined in this section, however, share the same weakness. Traditional measures of success are invariably financially based (for example, GDP or profitability – at economy and entity level, respectively). As such, the development of alternative measures of success will only be effective in terms of changing behaviour if they are more powerful than these tradition measures. Recognition of this potential weakness in the use of indicators has lead to approaches to SD evaluation that combine all elements into one measurement base (including that of money) and it is to these approaches that attention now turns.

Modelling for SD evaluation using a common metric

This approach is an extension of using indicators sets with decision rules to create a common measurement unit or score. Rather than come up with an abstract number from a multi-criteria decision tool, a common metric is used which has some traction in the minds of those using it. The three main common metrics are energy (or some energy measure such as emergy), land and money with each of these having particular implications.

A focus on energy arises from our current dependency on polluting forms of energy. As a result, measuring activities in terms of their energy impact is a way of pointing towards relative impact on global warming. If a system (a country or a company), event (such as a sports tournament) or product could be described in terms of its energy intensity you would get a proxy for its environmental performance (as one element of its SD performance). This rationale is behind desires to provide energy information on, for example, food labels (see, for example, Department for Environment, Food and Rural Affairs, 2005b and www.sustainweb.org) which communicate to consumers the energy used to grow, process and transport the product they are buying.

Land, in terms of space appropriated for particular uses, is also used in SD evaluations. Most usually this is expressed as an ecological footprint which indicates how much land is required to support the activities of a person, city or country. Land is used because it is a visually powerful way to communicate impact to individuals (the pedagogic value of the ecological footprint is noted by Costanza, 2000). It is also a powerful common currency because land is a finite resource (although land quality is not) and measuring lifestyles in this manner brings inequalities in land appropriation into sharp contrast and also highlights the extent to which the current ecological capacity of the planet is being exhausted (see Loh, 2000, who calculate that the ecological footprint of the world's population was at least 30% larger than the total biologically productive land available).

The final choice, that of money, is dictated by the observation that money currently drives perceptions of success and failure as well as decision-making activities. Thus, monetisation seeks to translate SD consequences of decisions into a language which can be presented alongside traditional decision-making tools. The last two approaches will now be illustrated as there is relevant recent experimentation in these areas (whereas energy accounting seems not to be currently used within social and environmental accounting, although is behind energy efficiency ratings and product labelling debates).

The most common composite indicators of impacts (using land as a metric) are ecological footprints (see Wackernagel and Rees, 1996) which are defined as the 'area of productive land and water ecosystems required to produce the resources that a population consumes and assimilate the wastes that the population produces' (Rees, 2000). In very simplistic terms, an ecological footprint is calculated by translating consumption (of food, housing, transport, consumer goods and services) into land use impacts. Land use impacts encompass 'built-up areas (supporting roads, housing and other infrastructure), crop land and pasture (for production of food and other goods), managed forests (for production of wood products) and energy land (for sequestering carbon dioxide emissions resulting from the burning of fossil fuels)' (McDonald and Patterson, 2004, p. 51). The outcome of such a calculation, combined with population and consumption data for each category of land use and adjusting for imports and exports, yields an average annual consumption per person of a physical land unit: usually expressed in the number of hectares required to support the lifestyle of the people in question. Rankings of countries and/or regions can then be developed from such an analysis.

The final approach to using a common measurement metric that will be examined here is the use of money. The current 'rules of the game', in both macro and micro level assessments of performance, rest on monetary estimations of whether or not we are doing 'better' or 'worse'. GDP, for example, is most usually seen as an indicator of the relative success of an economy (with higher levels of GDP being considered to be better). This is evident, for example, in the UK Government's approach to SD until 2005 in that one of the goals of SD was deemed to be 'high and stable levels of economic growth' (Department for Environment, Transport and the Regions, 1999). The perception of GDP being unquestioningly 'good' for SD, however, is shifting. Evidence for this can be found in the UK Government's most recent articulation of SD (Department for Environment, Food and Rural Affairs, 2005a) where creating a sustainable economy is articulated (albeit that what a sustainable economy may look like in 'reality' is not spelled out). There are, however, a number of attempts in the public domain to describe how you could tell if an economy was creating welfare (which itself would be a necessary but not sufficient step to describing what an economy which met the criteria of SD would be).

The two main approaches to establishing a monetary indicator of what could be seen to approximate SD performance for a country's economy are the Index of Sustainable Economic Welfare (ISEW, see, for more detail, Jackson and Marks, 1994) and the Genuine Progress Indicator (GPI, see, for more detail, Cobb et al., 1989). Both of these indicators use similar methods to 'correct' measures of GDP so that it may be seen to be more akin to a measure of welfare and may, therefore, be a measure of relative SD performance. These are not the only approaches. The World Bank uses a measure which it terms 'genuine savings' which takes traditional economic measures of savings reduced by measures of resource depletion and environmental degradation with increases in human capital added to it. Likewise, some countries (notably the Netherlands) have developed satellite environmental accounts which complement their system of national accounts and thereby attempt to measure ecologically sustainable economic activity.

To be more explicit, GDP measures the economic activity undertaken within an economy which is reflected in markets in some way. GDP does not distinguish what makes up the sum of these economic transactions and as such it does not measure the welfare of a country. In addition, activities which enhance welfare but which are not part of the economy (for example, unpaid work provided in the household, in raising children, supporting partners in work and caring for ill or old people) are not reflected in GDP but clearly enhance society's welfare. To illustrate these points: if a country has a large pollution event then the costs associated with dealing with the disaster result in GDP rising above what it would have been the absence of the event as the economic cost of cleaning up works its way through the economy. The event, therefore, will increase GDP, while most people are likely to view such an event as a negative event for a country, its population and the environment. In a similar vein, the extraction of oil is added to the sum of GDP as it costs to extract, process, consume and deal with the pollution that arises from this process whereas from an SD perspective it could be seen as a loss of a physical resource base and thus detrimental to the welfare of future generations. As a result, under GDP, non-renewable resource extraction is seen as a positive while under these alternative measures of welfare it is viewed as a loss of non-renewable resources (while recognising that it is used to generate positive outcomes such as providing heating and mobility).

The interest in alternative measures of performance thus arises from a belief that GDP, while measuring a certain array of activity in an economy, does not measure welfare. Certainly from an SD perspective, GDP is seen as being blind to the social and environmental

Table 2.4: Adjustments made to GDP to obtain the GPI

GDP

− costs of crime and family breakdown/divorce
+ value of household and volunteer work (childcare, home repairs, volunteer work).

Adjust for income distribution (+when poor receive larger percentage of national income, − when their share decreases)
- resource depletion (including habitat destruction and use of non-renewable resources)
- pollution costs
- estimates of long-term environmental damage (focusing on climate change costs, the costs of dealing with nuclear wastes and the use of ozone depleting substances).

Adjust for the amount of leisure time people have (+when leisure time rises, − when leisure time falls)
- defensive expenditures (money spent to prevent misfortune. For example, medical and accident repair costs, pollution control devices and commuting costs).

Adjustment for life of assets purchased (costs of purchase are deducted while value of service provided is added on). Thus a long-lived consumer product would increase GPI over time while something which is designed to wear out quickly would not do so.

Adjust for borrowing from abroad and the use of funds. If a country borrows money from abroad GPI reduces, when money (regardless of its source) is used to invest in a country's infrastructure the GPI increases. As a result, GPI is better when a country uses its own resources to fund investment. Borrowing money from abroad to fund consumption now creates a negative effect

= GPI.

For more information see www.redefiningprogress.org.

impacts of economic behaviour and hence the ISEW and the GPI could be viewed as SD orientated evaluations. Interest in alternative measures of success is given a further boost because GDP is seen by the majority of policy makers as an indicator which should grow over time and as a result government policies that are aimed at boosting GDP. Such policies, however, are not always likely to result in improvements to the SD performance of a country. The ISEW and the GPI both take GDP as the basis for analysis and then adjust for various elements. Table 2.4 outlines the basic adjustments which are made to transform GDP to the GPI.

The ISEW (for more information see www.foe.co.uk, which also includes a facility to calculate your own ISEW and review GDP versus ISEW for a number of countries) is similar to the GPI. It also adds to GDP non-market labour services (household and volunteer work) and then deducts loss of natural capital, pollution and environmental damage and personal costs of consumption. The extent to which the two differ need not detain us here as it is the principles of their calculation rather than the detail which is of most relevance. What they both seek to do in broad terms is to identify and quantify externalities (both positive in the form of unpaid labour and negative in terms of environmental damage) of countries.

Similar principles to those outlined here also arise in monetary modelling of SD at the level of an enterprise or project, and it is to these experiments that attention now turns. It is also within these approaches that the Sustainability Assessment Model (SAM) sits. In a similar manner to the ISEW and GPI, micro level evaluations of SD focus on the extent to which conventional measures of success (invariably profitability in the case of organisations) fail to capture all externalities from a defined arena of activity and attempt to 'deflate' the profit measure by those externalities. Various attempts to do this have been made under the broad heading of FCA (see Bebbington et al., 2001 for a fuller introduction to this technique and its application).

The impetus for FCA arose from the call in 1992 for accounting techniques to be developed which would ensure that 'the consumption and use of [in this case] environmental resources are accounted for as part of the full cost of production and reflected in market prices' (European Commission, 1992, Vol. II, p. 67). Over the last 10–15 years there have been a number of attempts to operationalise FCA. Most of these attempts have focused on environmental externalities and are hence not full accounts of SD performance. They are, however, the starting point for such accounts and the main experiments are outlined in Table 2.5.

All of these experiments follow the same basic format: (1) a cost objective is defined (as a project, an activity or an entity); (2) the scope of the analysis is defined (that is, what externalities are to be addressed are determined); (3) the impacts of the cost objective is quantified in physical/environmental terms (for example, in terms of resources used or emissions generated) and (4) these impacts are then monetised in some manner and (most usually) related to traditional financial information to generate some 'net' measure of profitability.

Table 2.5: Prior monetised experiments

BSO/Origin

Calculated 'environmental value added' by taking profits and subtracting from them the costs of reducing their environmental impact to a level that accorded with the Netherlands Government's expectations of what would be 'acceptable' levels of pollution (drawn from the Dutch National Environmental Plan). Macro level policy priorities were thus translated into entity specific costs which would be incurred if the entity were to meet these national targets. The aim of experiment was to provide an order of magnitude of the costs of being environmentally unsustainable. Figures were calculated for 1990–1994 inclusive. Even with attention to managing impacts BSO/Origin found that per employee impact initially fell (by approximately 30%) but then became static. Total impact rose over time as the entity's activity base increased.

Ontario Hydro (see also United States Environmental Protection Agency, 1996)

Calculated selected health and environmental impacts of fossil fuel generation of electricity with the impetus for this work being the need to charge the full costs for electricity produced in Canada but exported to the USA. It was also suggested that undertaking FCA provided incentives to search for the most economic ways of reducing environmental damage and more efficient and effective entity performance. It is not clear that this latter outcome was achieved and this experiment ceased when the organisation had a change in CEO.

Manaaki Whenua/Landcare Research (New Zealand) Ltd and the sustainable cost calculation (see also Bebbington and Gray, 2001)

Attempted to determine what additional costs would be borne by the organisation if it were to return the biosphere to the point it was at the beginning of an accounting period. Thus, this experiment focused on measuring environmental impact from activities and imputing remediation costs of these impacts. The problems in operationalising such a vision and the limitations facing a single organisation as it seeks to reduce its impact was highlighted by the experiment.

Forum for the Future (see also www.forumforthefuture.org.uk for more information)

A number of large companies (including Interface Europe, Anglian Water and Wessex Water) have worked with Forum for the Future to estimate their 'sustainability cost'. For a subset of environmental impacts the experiment estimated how much would have to be spent to either avoid or mitigate the impacts and this amount is deducted from the profit measure for the period.

In addition, more recent work (see Bent, 2004) regarding social externalities of alcohol consumption are modelled with avoidance and remediation costs again being estimated. In this latter work avoidance and remediation costs are compared with each other to determine, roughly speaking, 'what you get for your money' if you sought to address social externalities.

Source: Drawn from Bebbington et al. (2001), Chapter 5 unless otherwise indicated.

All FCA experiments, therefore, will have underlying them a set of indicators. The key difference between using indicators with assessment and monetary approaches, therefore, is that the assessment step is achieved via monetisation. Any judgements made about combining aspects of impacts is thus tied up in the monetisation approach and is less visible to users and less easy to grasp. In addition, the monetisation step in FCA is the most contentious on two grounds. First, for many monetisation it is morally repugnant as excessive focus on monetisation gives rise to externalities in the first place. Adding more calculative rationality to the problem is therefore seen as being counterproductive. Second, the monetisation step is technically the most difficult: both in terms of finding data from the economics literature that will allow monetisation and also for the fact that different ways of generating data for monetisation will yield very different figures to FCA calculations. As a result, while FCA provides a challenge to conventional measures of success using the tools of financial analysis, the figures generated are hard to interpret with any certainty. In the majority of instances where FCA has been attempted, however, the process of making the judgements called for and the thinking through of the link between cost objective and externalities is seen as immensely valuable in itself. This experience is echoed in the case of the SAM (as an example of FCA) as well.

Conclusions

In summary, this chapter has sought to describe three broad approaches to SD performance measurement with practical examples of each approach being provided. Each approach has its own strengths and weaknesses, and it is fair to say that none of the examples described are perfect in their conception or execution. What each approach attempts to do, however, is usually fourfold. First, most approaches seek to make transparent the various interactions which arise in the system under examination and make explicit how actions and/or choices drive external environmental (and social) impacts. This is especially valuable as in the most part we are ignorant of the impacts of actions and choices. The approaches, therefore, assist in educating us about the nature and scale of our current unsustainability. Second, whatever approach is adopted (in general or in particular) one would hope it provides a consistent measure of SD performance. This would enable trends in performance over time to be observed. In addition, the SD performance profile of various activities may be benchmarked against each other if a consistent approach is undertaken. Third, the aim of SD approaches is to enable decisions to be made on the basis of the information generated. Given the current stage of development of some of these tools this is a difficult goal to satisfy completely. Of the tools described, however, the IA multi-criteria analysis is perhaps the one which has been used most systematically to inform decisions. In addition, the various indicators projects show promise in this respect. Finally, one would hope, to a greater or lesser extent, that the approaches described would enable individuals to participate in discussions about SD performance on the basis of the data presented. These generic aims also underlie the development of the SAM and it is to this particular method of monetised modelling that attention turns to in Chapter 3.

The Sustainability Assessment Model: An Outline and Evaluation

Introduction

To date two tasks have been undertaken. First, the background to the importance of sustainable development (SD) as a public policy goal has been sketched along with examples of how various bodies are seeking to incorporate SD imperatives in their operations. A key element to the process of pursuing SD is developing some way to account for SD performance: the second task undertaken to date. In this context a number of approaches were introduced including: indicators, indicators with evaluation and common metric modelling. As will be become apparent, the Sustainability Assessment Model (SAM) is an example of the latter approach, using the common metric of money. A set of economic, resource, environmental and social indicators underpin the SAM and these indicators are translated into monetary figures. In the case of the SAM, a decision rule is then applied to the resulting figures to determine the extent to which a project could be said to match the principles of SD. In order to outline the SAM this chapter contains two aspects. First, the background to the development of the SAM is provided. Understanding the goal of the SAM is important because its value can only be assessed against that original goal. The second element addressed in the chapter is a technical specification of the SAM itself.

Background to the SAM

The SAM was initiated by the SD co-ordinator at BP in 1999 as a way to ground that organisation's aspirations to pursue more sustainable forms of development. While there was a strategic focus on SD matters at the time of SAM's inception, there were no detailed operational mechanisms or procedures which were devoted specifically to ensuring that SD was achieved. That is not to say that SD-related issues were not considered. For example, operating a robust environmental management system and managing health and safety aspects of operations are elements of SD performance. To the extent to which these elements are managed by organisations then they could be said to be dealing with elements of SD performance. What was missing, however, is a specific focus on evaluatory tools for SD performance of activities as a whole and the SAM was initiated to fill this perceived gap.

BP's approach to SD performance evaluation was to focus on discrete projects. The reasons for this focus were twofold. In the first instance, given the nature of the industry (and given the nature of the physical resource which is to be exploited) oil and gas companies organise and control their activities on a project basis. Second, given that operations are organised around relatively discrete operational assets, existing evaluation and approval of activities also focus on projects (in this manner the SAM mapped onto existing organisational control routines). The operational basis of the organisation, therefore, led to the project being considered the most appropriate focus of evaluation and control. This is not to say that the project level would be the only basis of SD assessment of an organisation's activities. For example, an organisation's impact on SD in its totality is also an important level of analysis. In such an analysis, however, it is less easy to pinpoint specific causes of SD impacts and it is not likely to correspond with the mechanisms by which operational decisions are made.

A project focus, however, has limitations. First, if SD issues arise from the combined impacts of a number of projects then the SAM will not necessarily identify these impacts. This would especially be the case should a number of projects be operating within the same ecological space (such as the North Sea where there cumulative impact on marine life, for example, is possible). Second, there will be activities which an organisation undertakes outside of a project focus which will have impacts upon the pursuit of SD. The most obvious situation where this could arise is if an organisation is involved in lobbying activities to shape regulatory regimes in ways which could be positive or negative from an SD point of view. The shape of these various regimes will set the context for organisational performance and hence will have SD impacts. Third, and perhaps more crucially, if accounting for SD performance is linked to creating the possibility of holding organisations to account for their activities then a project evaluation focus will not provide the mechanism (on its own) for the exercise of this accountability. While the data from project evaluations could plausibly provide data for accountability (if all projects were combined together and if other actions outside of project activities were incorporated into an SD account) it is unlikely to be sufficient for this purpose. Is it likely, therefore, that the SAM will be more orientated towards management control than the discharge of accountability.

In addition to deciding that project appraisal would be a useful point at which to insert SD considerations, the cost demands of the SD tool was also an issue. The specification for the SAM was that it should be relatively easily understandable by all project team members, it should not take a long time to gather the data and it should be able to be run at minimum cost. Such requirements preclude extensive modelling of all possible SD impacts. It was required, therefore, that any SD tool would be able to generate a quick view of SD performance which, if appropriate, could prompt further investigations. The extent to which the tool engaged project members from all backgrounds was a crucial element in design. The resource requirement (in terms of time and money) resulted in materiality of impacts being an important consideration.

In summary, the SAM was developed by BP to articulate SD issues at the level of project evaluation. It was seen as potentially providing a mechanism by which SD issues could be articulated in a context that could affect operational decisions. As such, while it was motivated by a desire to create performance which was in accordance with SD imperatives, it was also seen as a possible way in which to educate employees about SD at a level of resolution which matched their operational responsibilities. From the outset, therefore, there were at least two objectives for the SAM: modelling and accounting for SD performance and creating a context within which individuals who would not otherwise think about SD could find out about the concept and its application to activities for which they were directly responsible. As will become apparent, this second objective (to engage thinking around SD issues) is perhaps the more important contribution of the SAM. Before coming to this point, however, more detail about the SAM itself is now provided.

Outline of the SAM

The SAM follows the 'standard' four step full cost accounting (FCA) approach: (1) define cost objective, (2) specify the scope of the analysis, (3) identify impacts of cost objective and (4) monetise impacts. In the first instance, the SAM defines the focus of the exercise (the cost objective) as being a discrete project guided by a project team for the reasons outlined above. The initial project on which the SAM was developed was an oil and gas field development and this example will be used to illustrate the functionality of the SAM.

Second, the boundaries of evaluation using the SAM were defined widely. In particular, the SAM tracks SD impacts of a project over its full life cycle. In the case of an oil and gas development this starts with exploration drilling, the design of (for example) a drilling and production platform, the construction, installation and commissioning of the platform, the production of oil and gas and the eventual decommissioning of the platform. These parts of an oil and gas development are (usually) directly controllable by a project management team. The SAM, however, extends the analysis beyond extraction of oil and gas and traces the impacts from refining, the manufacture of products from oil and gas and eventual product use. Thus the SAM examines cradle to grave impacts of an oil and gas field. The decision to have such a wide focus could appear to be at odds with a project evaluation focus. This is, however, not the case.

An assessment of an activity which ignores the upstream and downstream impacts of that activity could not be thought to fully address SD issues. Indeed, as will become apparent, in the case of an oil and gas field development, if the full life cycle impacts are not included in the analysis then the SD impact of the exploration and production phase are comparatively minimal. Further, the cradle to grave approach also demonstrates how the SAM does not neatly map into existing accountability relationships. For example, BP are not responsible (and therefore not accountable) for impacts of oil and gas combustion in motor vehicle travel. It may be the case, however, that actions taken at the production phase could have an impact on subsequent impact of the use of the product. While it is difficult to see how this is the case with respect to oil and gas production, it can more easily be seen in the design and manufacture of products where recycling at the end of a product's life is built in from the outset. In this instance, the downstream SD impact of a product/activity could be affected by actions taken before that point in time in the product chain. The principle of using full life cycle impacts, therefore, is a sound one.

The third aspect of the SAM has been to identify and measure the impacts of the project. Within the SAM, impacts are considered using four headings: economic, resource use, environmental and social.

These categories of impacts are determined from the focus of SD on the ecological and social outcomes of economic activity. In the case of ecological impacts a decision was made to separate out the implications of a project on resource availability as well as the pollution impacts of a project (which are covered under the environmental heading). The activity data from which to impute impact has been drawn from two sources. In the first instance, project data which is already gathered is used. For example, the hours worked on the project, number of people employed, expected number of barrels of oil produced, amount of water used, amount of materials used in fabrication, waste produced and estimates of the financial performance of the project represents data which is already gathered in the process of project evaluation. This activity data is then either used directly in the SAM or used to impute the economic, resource use, environmental or social impacts. For example, if one is examining environmental externalities over a full life cycle then the barrels of crude oil extracted from an oil and gas field development will, when combusted, result in certain air pollution impacts. In order to model the environmental impact of a project, the profile of air pollutant which will be generated from crude oil of a certain chemical composition has to be estimated for the SAM to be operational. This is an example of imputing environmental impacts.

In terms of identifying impacts it should be noted that all possible impacts have not been incorporated into the SAM. Rather, and in order to keep the exercise manageable, a handful of impacts (an upper limit of 25 items was set) are considered with the choice of impacts being driven by informed consideration of what would be likely to be the most significant impacts. Some impacts were considered and discarded (as being impossible to gather data on or were found to contribute little to the analysis) with the final set representing a 'best guess' of the significant impacts of an oil and gas field. Clearly, deciding at the outset what is likely to be important in terms of impact is an essential task. It may be, in order to maintain comparability, that similar categories of impact could be used by anyone organisation to evaluate all projects. Alternatively, each SAM could reflect the particular significant SD impacts of a project and this approach would seem to be the most robust approach to take. Each approach has pros and cons: on balance the latter approach was considered more useful. A considerable amount of discussion, therefore, is necessary at the start of a SAM to define the categories of impact which are most relevant for an SD evaluation.

The final step undertaken has been to monetise the SD impacts identified as arising from the development of the oil and gas field. In this manner, physical measures of impact are converted into a common measurement base, that of money (the rationale for monetisation was covered in Chapter 2). A variety of monetisation approaches have been adopted (and will be dealt with as each element of the SAM is described below) with current prices or the open literature being used as far as possible for identifying a monetisation mechanism.

In summary, the SAM follows a generic four-step approach to FCA. The focus of the model is on a discrete project with the boundary of analysis being cradle to grave. Impacts are quantified in physical terms and then monetised using a variety of methods. What is being modelled is the outcome of a transformative event (in this case the development and use of an oil and gas field) as it affects various capital categories. In broad terms the transformation process in exploiting an oil and gas field is that natural resource (the oil and gas) is transformed into economic benefits (for the firm extracting the oil and gas) and social benefits (in the form of mobility, heating and products produced from the oil and gas). At the same time, social costs (for example, costs of mobility such as road deaths and congestion costs) and environmental costs (for example, global warming impacts from combustion of fossil fuel) also occur. The SAM, therefore, seeks to model the changes in capitals (economic, resource, environmental and social) which arise from the transformative activity. The following sections outline in more detail each capital element within the SAM.

Economic flows

The economic flows recorded in the SAM are the most recognisable to accountants, but even here there is uncertainty in the data. Flows under the heading of economic represent the total economic benefit which accrues from the project to the entity for which the SAM is being calculated. For an oil and gas project total benefit is measured by the total barrels of crude which will be generated by the development multiplied by the estimated crude selling price over the life of the project (with both of these numbers clearly being estimates).

These figures will be captured in the accounting systems of the organisation over the life of the project and are therefore the non-externalities of the project, from the point of view of the organisation.

The total revenue from a field can be split in any manner which is helpful to the organisation undertaking the exercise. In the case of BP, total revenue was split according to who receives the income: shareholders (via dividends), government (via taxation), operators (via capital and revenue spending on the project), social investments made by the project and BP (for the amount which is reinvested in the business). The relationship between the amounts of money going to these various recipients was used to determine the viability of a project using conventional accounting measures (such as payback period and internal rate of return). Further, while these flows will have resource, environmental and social impacts, these impacts are not captured under this category of flows unless there is a direct payment for an impact. The remaining impacts identified, therefore, represent the external impacts from the underlying economic activity: that is, the rest of the SAM seeks to describe the externalities that arise from the project.

Resource use flows

The resource category in the SAM attempts to capture the value of resources used, to the extent that payments made (and captured under economic flows) do not fully account for the use of resources. Such a distinction is necessary to ensure that double counting is avoided. In theory, economists value environmental change arising from resource use on the basis of the 'economic rent of depleted resources' (Ekins, 2000, p. 12) which is itself estimated in a variety of ways (net price approach, present value approach or user cost method). There is no consensus as to which approach is the correct one. What is clear, however, is that one important aspect of resource use is that once used the resource cannot be used in the future for an alternative, possibly more valuable use.

Resources identified in the SAM are: oil and gas (the principle category given the nature of the project), water, energy, raw materials, intellectual capital and infrastructure. These resources represent a negative externality (that is an overall external cost) as the net effect of their use is to reduce the array of resources available for future use.

The example of oil and gas, which constitutes the largest impact for this application of the SAM, will be used to demonstrate the reasoning. The physical measure of the resource which will no longer be available after this project is the estimated number of barrels of crude in the reservoir (noting that this figure is never known for sure). The total volume of a reservoir is invariably less than the number of barrels of crude which are sold under the economic element of the project. This apparent mismatch is due to the fact that once a reservoir has been exploited, under current operating rules, it will not be revisited (for technical and economics reasons) and hence the resource is left in the ground and unavailable for use by future generations. For this resource, therefore, we have a pattern where actual barrels extracted underlie the economic, environment and social capital categories but where total barrels in the reservoir are reflected in the resource section. For oil and gas the physical units in the reservoir are multiplied by an opportunity cost figure for oil and gas. This figure is the lost value to society of not having the resource, over and above the price which is paid by BP to acquire the resource. Having noted that the overall effect is a negative impact there are positive flows within this sub-category as well (for example, where a project can be seen to develop intellectual capital of individuals or the organisation) which offsets the overall negative figures. There is, as a result, a 'bounce' effect within this category with both positive and negative externalities being netted off against each other.

Environmental flows

Environmental externalities (which are again negative figures for an oil and gas development) arise primarily from the environmental damage incurred by the use of oil and gas resources. While resource use and environmental damage are both categories of impact which fall on the natural environment, due to the different nature of these impacts the SAM identifies the impacts separately. In addition, given the oil and gas industry is an extractive industry the (in some ways artificial) separation of impacts is useful to project evaluation. In particular, the degree of control which a project exercises over resource impacts is higher than that of environmental damage. For example, the reservoir recovery ratio is within the control of the project (while noting that ultimately this is under the control of the geology of the reservoir). In contrast, the pollution impact from final product use of oil and gas products, such as in transportation, is not controllable by the project team.

The SAM includes four categories of environmental impact: impacts from emissions to the atmosphere (including emissions from product use); depreciation of properties which arise from noise, odour and visual nuisance related to the project; land area unavailable for use due to installations (which is termed footprint and includes an exclusion zone around oil and gas platforms in which fishing is not permitted for safety reasons) and impacts of waste created in the process of developing an oil and gas field. The first and last categories of impact are the most significant for an oil and gas field development.

In physical terms, once the chemical composition of an oil and gas reservoir is known the pollution which will arise, for example on combustion, can be estimated. Hence we have a chain of data from the physical units of the resource, via a calculation of air pollution which will arise from combustion of the oil/gas to an estimate of the financial costs of the air pollution. This last step involves two additional layers of modelling and is tied up in the damage cost figures which are used (taking the example of greenhouse gas emissions) to convert tonnes of carbon dioxide emitted into a monetary estimation of its cost. First, the impact of the pollution has to be modelled and then the economic value of the damage is estimated. There are a variety of methods for creating damage costs, the figures used in the SAM are BP's own damage cost assessments (see Bebbington et al., 2001, p. 65 for a discussion of various valuation methods). These figures are within the range of figures which exist in the open literature, most usually in government sponsored publications of the damage costs of pollution (see, for example, European Commission, 1995; Samson et al., 2001).

Social flows

Modelling the social flows from an oil and gas field development was the most difficult aspect of the construction of the SAM. There are three elements which are captured under this heading and which combine (that is, there are positive and negative externalities) to create a net positive social benefit. The three elements are: the external impact of employment, how a project contributes more broadly to creating a socially sustainable society and the social impact of the products which arise from oil and gas field development.

Social externalities of employment have both positive and negative aspects to them. The positive externality of employment is the multiplier effect which arises from employment whereby wages paid to individuals during the project are spent by employees and thereby support the local economy. There are well-established methodologies for determining what a £1 spent in a particular location will generate in terms of positive externalities. This benefit is offset by the negative impact of deaths and accidents which arise during employment on the project. The costs of deaths and accidents are those costs which are deemed to exist above those costs paid by the entity itself (for example, in compensation to employees or their families). As a result, there is, once again, a 'bounce' effect in the model with pluses and minuses to capital categories existing (the possibilities for offsetting these are discussed later).

The second element under social impact sought to identify how a project could be seen to contribute to a socially sustainable society. Problems arose in operationalising this idea for two reasons: what constitutes a socially sustainable society is itself difficult to determine and the connections between a project and aspects of a social sustainability were not clear. It was believed, however, that it was important to try to consider this aspect. As a result, this part of the SAM draws from the (now previous) United Kingdom (hereafter UK) Government's Strategy on SD (Department for Environment, Transport and the Regions, 1999) to outline the characteristics of a socially sustainable society. The headline indicators from the UK Strategy were examined and all those indicators which had an explicit social orientation and which were not captured in any other part of the SAM were identified. This resulted in examination of four categories that, if improving, would lead to a more socially sustainable society. The categories are: tackling poverty and social exclusion, equipping people with the skills to fulfil their potential, reducing the proportion of unfit housing stock and reducing both crime and the fear of crime. All the other headline indicators found parallels somewhere in the SAM. For example, the 'prudent use of natural resources' is considered within the resource leg of the SAM; air pollution goals are inherent in the environmental impact category; and 'maintain high and stable levels of economic growth' can be seen to be reflected under the economic leg and in the jobs multiplied in the social category. As a result, the SAM has been 'sense checked' against what was deemed at the time to be the issues which were crucial for SD in the UK. This provides further reassurance that the categories of impacts chosen are defendable in some manner. In identifying these four social residual categories, the SAM suggests that if a project results in impacts upon these indicators then it will affect (in either a positive or negative manner) the socially sustainability profile of the project. The difficulty then faced is how to identify a link between a project and these indicators.

For an oil and gas field development in the North Sea, it proved very difficult to make any direct linkages between the above indicators and project performance. An indirect link between the project and social impacts was sought with the taxation paid over the life of a project being used as the linking factor. Specifically, taxation spend by the Government will impact upon the indicators of social sustainability listed and the project contributes to the funding available for Government spending and is, therefore, indirectly linked to social sustainability. In order to make the link, the total taxation paid is pro-rated by Government spending category (for example, health, education and transportation) using data published by the Treasury. The benefit arising from spending in each category is then estimated. For example, the question asked is: for each pound spent by the Government on health, what social benefit (in financial terms) is generated by the expenditure? A mix of data sources have been used for these factors drawing from economic studies in the public domain. In some instances, a variety of data sources have been used to determine the impact of taxation spend. An example may be informative here.

In seeking to link taxation spend to positive social externalities which could be generated from that spending the following steps were undertaken. First, the British crime survey puts the cost of crime at £60 billion per year for England and Wales (grossing this amount up for the UK as a whole, gives a cost of £65 billion). While it was impossible to estimate how much crime is avoided by the spending on law, order and protective services we do know how much was spent on policing (some £9.8 billion in 2000/2001). In addition, it was noted from performance league tables that police solved 25% of all reported crime. It is, therefore, broadly plausible to imagine that the existence of a police force also prevented 25% of all possible crime which could have taken place. Once that assumption is made, it is possible to guess at a social benefit of taxation spent on ensuring law and order (with this being linked to the headline SD indicator of reducing both crime and fear of crime). Thus, if £65 billion constitutes 75% of all crime which could have taken place total crime would have cost society £87 billion. A £9.8 billion investment in policing, therefore, may have 'saved' £22 billion (£87 − £65 billion) of crime and as a result for every pound spent the social benefit is 2.25 times as much. As is apparent from this estimate, these are very rough and ready calculations, in the absence of information which would more directly answer the question we posed in this element of social impacts.

It was decided at the outset of developing the SAM to model a project's contribution to a sustainable society but at that time it was not known whether or not these categories of impact would be significant. Given they are not significant in the overall SAM signature (see Figure 3.1) then any errors of magnitude do not appear to affect the overall conclusions which could be drawn from the SAM and as a result, the 'roughness' of the approach suffices for now. At the same time, this would be an argument for excluding these impacts altogether from the SAM. There was a reluctance to do this because it was believed that in other jurisdictions the impact from taxation spending may be greater. In any event, conceptually, it was useful to keep this category of impact in the SAM.

The final category of social impact identified in the SAM is the social impact of the products (which are mobility, heating and petrochemical based products such as pharmaceuticals). The following explanation of how these figures were calculated focuses on mobility, but the principles are applicable to all oil and gas products. Given the SAM is a full life cycle model, the external costs of mobility (which is a major use of oil and gas) have been reflected in the model in terms of resource use and pollution impact from combusting oil and gas. At the same time, the economic category within the SAM captures the value of oil and gas by reference to the price paid for crude oil. As a result, there is a need to capture the value which society places on mobility in excess of the price of crude, but also taking into account any adverse social consequences of mobility. The social impacts of products are therefore a combination of two factors, one positive and one negative. The positive factor relates to the difference between the crude price and the current selling price of fuel which measures the market's best estimate of the value which people assign to mobility (and which was inflated in the SAM due to fuel being relatively price inelastic). The negative factor is the social costs of mobility which are not identified anywhere else in the SAM. These costs relate primarily to the cost of congestion and road accidents (with data being drawn from Samson et al., 2001). The resulting figure is a net positive amount.

As is apparent from the above discussion the social impacts of a project have presented the greatest challenge in the development of the SAM and have involved the least certain cost and benefit estimation methods. At the same time, however, it is these social issues which dominate public policy discussions of the contribution which the oil and gas industry makes to society's pursuit of SD and as such we believe it is essential to have the issues represented in the SAM. Further, in terms of the quantum of external costs and benefits it is the social benefit of mobility which plays a large role in the shape of the SAM signature.

Bring the flows together and evaluating SD performance

The modelling of the transformations which an oil and gas project creates and the identification of what are the significant flows in that transformation process is only the starting point of the SAM analysis. Converting the various disparate flows into financial terms, however, does allow us to graph them together. Figure 3.1 represents the SAM 'signature' for a typical oil and gas field development (other types of development have different typical signatures) and will form the basis for further discussions about what the output of the SAM implies.

By way of explanation, all of the bars above the horizontal line in Figure 3.1 represent a positive benefit for a capital sub-category while all bars below the horizontal represent a disbenefit for a capital sub-category (as measured in monetary terms). The various shadings in each bar represent one element within the capital sub-category (as outlined above). The transformative process of an oil and gas field development is thus described by the signature: financial and social

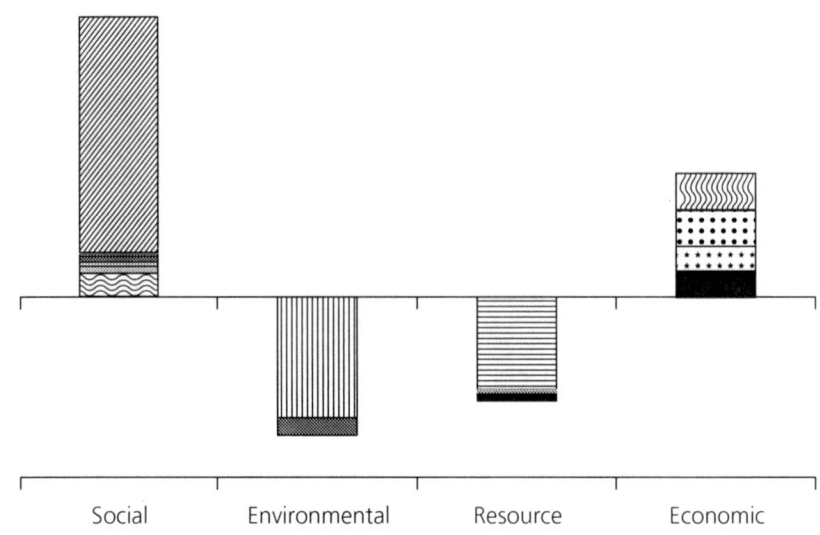

Figure 3.1 A SAM signature for a 'typical' oil and gas field development.

benefits are obtained at the expense of environmental and resource usage costs. The economic leg of the signature contains internalities (that is, they are reflected, over time, in the financial accounts of BP). The remaining elements are externalities (that is, these costs and benefits are experienced by other than the organisation who conducts the project).

It is also worth noting that the economic benefit is usually the only visible account of an oil and gas field development for the organisation which is undertaking the development. The signature, however, draws out the externalities (positive and negative) which arise over the full life cycle of an oil and gas field development. In addition, the major benefits and disbenefits of oil and gas field development (represented in the social and environmental sub-categories) arise after the oil and gas is extracted and are thus beyond the direct control of the organisation extracting the oil and gas, as well as being beyond the direct control of any one group in society. Furthermore, three aspects of the signature dominate all others: the use of oil and gas resources (the horizontal lines under resource use), air pollution impacts of combusting oil and gas (the vertical lines under environmental impact) and the social benefits arising from the product (which is the slanting lines under social impacts).

While an examination of the signature is instructive it may also be used in a more focused manner to tell a story about whether or not a particular development could be said to be an SD. In order to make such an assessment, some assumptions about the substitutability between different capital groups are necessary and further elaboration on this point is necessary.

We have noted that there are both positive and negative outcomes from an oil and gas field development. It would, therefore, be reasonable to assume that in each sub-category of capital where the number is positive, capital has been sustained and where the number is negative, capital has not been sustained. Further, it should be noted that SD is often conceptualised as requiring 'constancy of capital stock' (Gray and Bebbington, 2001, p. 306 quoting David Pearce, an influential UK economist). The conceptualisation behind the SAM mirrors closely this constancy of capitals focus.

Deciding if a particular SAM signature describes an SD, therefore, depends on the extent to which the capital sub-categories can be combined. The degree of combination itself depends on the extent to which you believe that capital is substitutable. There is a spectrum of views on this matter and these views will affect an evaluation of whether or not a project could be said to be sustainable in terms of its SAM signature. At one end of the spectrum, if all capital is assumed to be substitutable and if the sum of all elements of the SAM signature is positive, then the development could be said to be sustainable. It is, however, usually assumed that critical capital cannot be substituted. If this approach were to be taken then all capitals could be added together. The project, however, could not be seemed to be sustainable if it resulted in any loss of critical capital. As an aside, critical natural capital is made up of those elements of the biosphere which we have only one of. It is not always obvious what critical capital is. Species are often considered to be part of critical natural capital but in the context of oil and gas it is not clear if a stable climatic system is critical natural capital. If a stable climatic system is critical capital then the signature represented in Figure 3.1 would not constitute a sustainable project due to the air emission impacts of the oil and gas field.

A different position would be to allow substitution between elements within a capital sub-category but not to allow substitution between capital sub-categories. In this approach a project could be said to be sustainable if every sub-category had a net positive impact and if there was no loss in critical capital (however defined). Under such a decision rule one would tolerate, for example, road deaths, given the benefits which arise from mobility. Alternatively, it could be argued that no negative moves in capital could be tolerated (regardless of any benefits in a capital category) if a project was to be described as a sustainable project. A particular strength of the SAM is that it separates (as much as it is possible) the modelling of impacts and the evaluation of whether or not a project could be said to be sustainable. In this manner it attempts to provide a signature as the basis on which a discussion can be initiated. In this context there are a number of points which can be discussed further.

A number of issues are exercised here with respect to how the SAM may be used. These cover: (1) a further discussion on dealing with SD aspects that cannot be monetised, (2) using the SAM in 'what if' scenarios, (3) using one number of representing the SAM signature, (4) the possibilities for strategic use of the SAM and (5) what the SAM cannot tell you.

As noted above, the issue of critical natural capital is relevant to any assessment of SD, but it is an aspect which the SAM cannot adequately capture in financial terms. This arises because valuation of critical natural capital (once it is gone) is not a sensible notion. The nearest one could get to placing a monetary value on critical natural capital loss would be to assign it an infinitely negative number. While conceptually this is sound, how it could be presented alongside the SAM signature is problematic. In addition, there may be elements of impact which a project team identifies as being pertinent but which they cannot or are reluctant to place a monetary value on. For example, there could be an impact on indigenous communities for which monetisation was thought to be inappropriate. The problem then presents itself as to how these aspects which cannot be captured in the monetised signature should be represented along with it. Given the visual strength of the signature it would appear necessary to have these aspects alongside the signature. In this case we would suggest that items of the nature described here may be placed in 'bubbles' around the signature itself, should they be deemed to be important in the SD evaluation.

Once the SAM signature exists, it can be used to explore 'what if' scenarios. For example, if it was believed that it would be useful to undertake remediation in order to improve the SD signature of a project then the impact of remediation could be sketched using the SAM. For example, air emission impacts of transportation could be remediated by planting trees to soak up carbon emissions (noting that there are competing views on whether or not this would constitute remediation). Indeed, one project team who used the SAM decided to be carbon neutral with respect to all flights taken for planning and co-ordination purposes between the UK and the USA. In this instance the proposed remediation would reduce the damage costs under the environment bar. At the same time, overall the economic bar on the signature would remain the same with the split of the bar being affected by any remediation activities which involved the organisation outlaying money. Crudely speaking, a 'bang for your buck' would be evident from such a move and as long as the cost of remediating the impact is less than the damage cost, the SAM signature would improve (the SAM, however, is not a fully dynamic model of all interactions between a project and the economy).

To recap an earlier point, the resource leg reflects the loss of the whole oil and gas reservoir while the economic, environmental and social bars only reflect the oil and gas actually extracted. Given the ratio of cost (in terms of damage costs) to benefit (of mobility) implied by the signature, any improvement in the recovery rate of the oil and gas will improve the overall performance of the project. Naturally, such a move would also be economically attractive (at least up to a certain point) but even beyond that financial cutoff, improvements in recovery ratio would be beneficial from an SD perspective.

Another possibility which exists with respect to the signature is to collapse all the aspects down to a single figure. There are pros and cons of adopting such an approach. If several SAMs were being compared together and if some ranking of them were sought, then developing a single numerical representation of the combined outcome of the SAM may be useful. In this situation relative performance could be gauged (providing that the broad relationships between the numbers are not materially wrong). Likewise, developing a single figure to represent success or failure appears to be a deeply held human desire, as evidenced by the discussion in Chapter 2 about gross domestic product (GDP) and single measures. Using a capital substitution rule that a development must have all elements in the positive to be deemed to be sustainable but that positive and negatives in a single capital category can be tolerated, an index of the SAM (termed a SAM*i*) could be calculated by taking the sum of all categories (+ economic – resource – environmental + social) and dividing this by the absolute sum of all elements. In this way the net positive benefit as a percentage of total impact (both positive and negative) could be gauged. The nearer this figure is to 100% the more sustainable it could be said to be. In the case of the signature represented in Figure 3.1, the SAM*i* equates to 25%. Whether or not reducing the complexity of SD down into a SAM signature and then further reducing that down to a single number is useful is uncertain, yet it remains a possibility.

What is also possible is to use the SAM to focus on the key benefit of a project and to explore ways to enhance such a benefit while reducing the overall impact of the project. In Figure 3.1 the slanting lines represents the value of the products from society's perspective. Using the example of mobility, the SAM can be used to engage thinking beyond organisational boundaries about how less unsustainable forms of development may be pursued. The current SAM signature reflects the 'reality' of the 'rules of the game' as dictated by the current arrangements for obtaining mobility. If one is going to be mobile, most usually a motor vehicle is required into which fuel is put. Currently BP has a strong incentive to sell more fuel in order to make more profits. Unfortunately, such an approach also accelerates the negative environmental impacts of fuel (as demonstrated in the SAM). An alternative approach to the provision of mobility would be for individuals to buy 'mobility services' at a set cost for a set period of time. If a fuel provider, in partnership with a car manufacturer, could then provide mobility in a way which minimised the use of fuel, an incentive for doing so would exist. At this point the link between environmental damage and profit generation could be partially decoupled. The SAM makes this apparent in that the more mobility that you can achieve without resource use and pollution impact, the better the SAM signature will be. In this manner, the SAM may be used to prompt more strategic thinking with regard to how an organisation could seek to operate more closely in accordance with SD principles.

The final point which should be made with respect to the SAM is that the signature (of itself) cannot tell you what a sustainable world would look like. This is at least in part because in the transition to SD a great deal of things will change (especially market prices and economic valuations, on which the SAM is dependent). In addition, the SAM is itself a representation of relative unsustainability in an unsustainable economy (a point which Bebbington and Gray, 2001, also make). Thus, if one wanted to know what an SD will look like in the future, the SAM cannot necessarily tell you. In addition, a SAM on a project now will be different from a SAM on the same project in 10 years time because in the future not only will there be more complete data on actual operations, but the prices and economic valuations would have changed as well. The SAM, therefore, provides a glimpse of possible SD impacts for a discrete project now.

Conclusions

This chapter has outlined an approach to accounting for SD using a common metric, in this case that of money. The SAM provides a way of describing (in physical and then financial terms) the profile of a project and specially its impact on economic, resource, environmental and social capitals over a full life cycle. The transformative process which arises from a project is modelled with the most significant aspects of the transformation being quantified, monetised and used to develop the SAM signature. The signature is then used as the basis from which to evaluate the extent to which a project could be argued to be a sustainable project. How the SAM signature is used within detailed project appraisals depends on normative choices being made with respect to substitutability of capital. In this respect, modelling and evaluation of SD are separated.

While the SAM is a simple heuristic for capturing elements of SD, it is worth reiterating the original motivation for its development. BP sought to develop a project evaluation tool which provided information to project teams in a cost effective and timely manner. It was never the intention to provide a perfect model of all SD impacts of a project and to evaluate them in great depth in each instance. Rather, a quick but relatively robust approach to providing an SD snapshot which would engage thinking around SD within project teams was desired. Given the key elements of the SAM have now been presented, the next chapter outlines the various SAM runs which have been completed by BP and uses these to further consider how well this tool 'works' at the task which has been set for it.

Sustainability Assessment
Model in Action

Introduction

This chapter undertakes three tasks. In the first instance, a brief outline of BP's approach to project appraisal is provided in order to
place the Sustainability Assessment Model (SAM), its development
and use in context. Second, the use of the SAM (as described in
Chapter 3) by BP in a variety of different projects is outlined with the
SAM signatures from these projects being presented and discussed.
This part of the chapter is designed to demonstrate the way in which
the SAM has been used and examining the cases will further bring
out the functionality of the tool. The third part of the chapter provides an evaluation of the SAM, drawing from a variety of formal and
informal settings in which the SAM has been presented. This feedback has been elicited from those within BP who have used the tool
as well as from external parties who have interest and expertise in
sustainable development (SD) performance evaluation (including
accounting). As a result, by the end of this chapter the functionality
of the SAM and views on the efficacy of this particular approach to
SD evaluation will have been presented. This material then forms the
springboard for examining SD evaluation in other organisations both
within and outside of the oil and gas industry.

Project appraisal and capital budgeting in BP

This section briefly outlines BP's approach to project appraisal in the
context of capital budgeting. Such an outline is necessarily in order
to understand the context within which the SAM was developed
and also sheds light on potential uses of the SAM. This part of the
work also links to Chapter 5 where other oil and gas companies
were interviewed with the aim of generating similar insights.

A multi-stage process is used by BP to move from identifying an
opportunity, evaluating the viability of that opportunity to undertaking the activities necessary to complete the project. At each stage
of the process there is the requirement to pass through a 'gate'. This
entails presenting a business case for the project to a group of 'gatekeepers' (which, in the joint venture environment, includes partners).
In this respect the control of a project does not rest entirely with an
operator, but has to be jointly agreed among all partners to a project.
There are decision support packages at each stage of evaluation

which specify minimum requirements for information to be presented (for example, financial, health and safety, and environmental information). In addition, there are requirements to evaluate aspects of performance for which no set procedures are required. In this case, project teams will search BP's intranet to see what decision support tools have been used in the past and hence what may be useful for their purposes. Such an approach is consistent with a decentralised organisation who organises itself via compliance with targets and a strong performance review culture.

In this process, the SAM could become used in two ways. First, write ups of the 'lessons learned' from experimenting with the SAM could end up on the intranet and be picked up by other teams for use. Alternatively, if someone wished to champion SAM they may seek to communicate their enthusiasm about the tool via networks or distribution lists of interested people (environmental champions, for example). At a formal level, if the SAM was deemed to be a necessary part of the decision support package then it could be formally required for all projects (this is not currently the case, bearing in mind the 'compulsory' set of tools are quite small). As a result, there are both formal and informal networks through which information on the SAM could be obtained. In such a context, therefore, it becomes crucial that various experiences with SAM are communicated and it is to the various SAM experiments that this chapter now turns.

SAM in action: the cases

Three applications of the SAM will be discussed here. First, the production of the SAM for an oil and gas field development will be represented. Largely this is a reiteration of material from Chapter 3, as an oil and gas field development was used to develop the SAM template. The SAM, however, was run on several different oil and gas fields and a variety of results were obtained. In addition, an attempt to see if the SAM could distinguish performance by changing extraction approaches was undertaken. The oil and gas SAM template is then used to put the other two SAM experiments in context.

Oil and gas projects

Several SAM runs were developed on hydrocarbon projects and they all resulted in the same shape of signature (see Figure 4.1). The

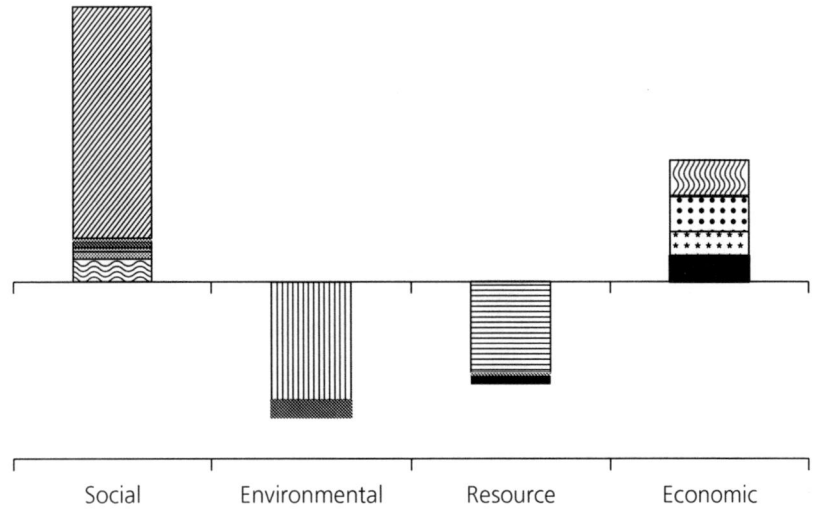

Figure 4.1 Hydrocarbon based SAM.

index of the SAM (SAM*i*) score, however, varied from a low of 25%
through to a high of 35% over the various projects. The best of these
projects (as judged by having a higher SAM*i*) was a gas development. In this case the pollution impact for energy made available
from the development was such that a better signature and score
were achieved. In addition, the recovery ratio on a project played a
pivotal role in the SAM profile achieved. The lowest score was
obtained by a project where a fractured geology leads to a relatively
low reservoir recovery ratio.

An observation on the SAM emerged in the context of a compara-
tive assessment of the oil and gas SAMs. A presentation of the SAM
was made to the project team which 'scored' a SAM*i* of 25% and a
note of the other SAM*is* were provided. This led to a heated discussion as to how the 25% scoring project team could improve
their score and hence outperform other projects. This discussion
took place regardless of the fact that the presentation has emphasised the uncertainties in the data and the problems of believing
that one number could appropriately capture project performance.
There are two conclusions which could be drawn from this observation. First, the tendency of individuals to focus on a single measure was reinforced by the way in which this project team focused

on the 'bottom line', as they saw it, of their SD performance. Second, the extent to which tools motivate performance should not be underestimated. This was the presentation of an experimental snapshot of performance, yet it still motivated individuals to rethink the design of their project. This experience suggests that the SAM can effectively engage individuals in conversations about project performance regardless of the 'rightness' of the numbers.

In addition to describing SAMs for oil and gas projects, there was also an attempt to see if the SAM had the functionality to distinguish between different design concepts. For one project, three different concepts were considered: (1) a twin steel jackets structure, (2) a steel floating platform design or (3) a concrete substructure. The results from each option are recorded in Table 4.1 (all have a signature similar to that in Figure 4.1).

Table 4.1 indicates the relative contribution of each capital category to overall performance (social − environmental − resource + economic = SAMi, recalling that the SAMi in this case represents the sum of all categories as a percentage of the absolute sum). Using this type of table highlights the relative performance of each option. It is, therefore, evident that the lower economic contribution from the floating platform concept drives the SAMi (as a consequence of the lower production and reserves delivery of this approach). Correspondingly the environment damage from the floating platform is lower since there is a smaller decommissioning impact than the other concepts. The concrete substructure concept shows a higher social benefit due to increased jobs during the construction phase of the development. The steel jacket concept shows the highest economic impact since this concept is the most commercial attractive having

Table 4.1: SAM for design decisions

Design concept	Social	Environmental	Resource	Economic	SAMi
		Each element as a percentage of total bar chart area			
Steel jacket	42.9	−21.0	−16.6	19.4	24.7
Steel floating platform	42.1	−20.9	−18.0	19.1	22.3
Concrete substructure	43.0	−20.9	−16.7	19.3	24.7

the highest net present value. While this exercise was considered useful, the SAM's functionality with respect to comparing different projects is likely to yield more valuable information from evaluating different types of projects. This can be seen from the following two projects which encompass different types of activities.

Landfill gas for energy project

Figure 4.2 presents the SAM signature for a project which sought to develop energy from landfill gas. The crucial point to note on this project is that the landfill already existed and hence the comparison point for the SAM signature was: what will the world look like (in terms of capital transformations) if landfill gas is collected for energy compared to the situation where the gas is left to be emitted into the atmosphere in the form of methane. This project definition is crucial to understanding this SAM signature, where the environment leg has become positive (in comparison to negative in the oil and gas field developments). The environmental element becomes positive in this case because methane has a higher warming potential than its component parts after combustion. This does not mean that landfill constitutes an SD, nor does Figure 4.2 describe the SAM for a decision as to whether or not to have landfill (regardless

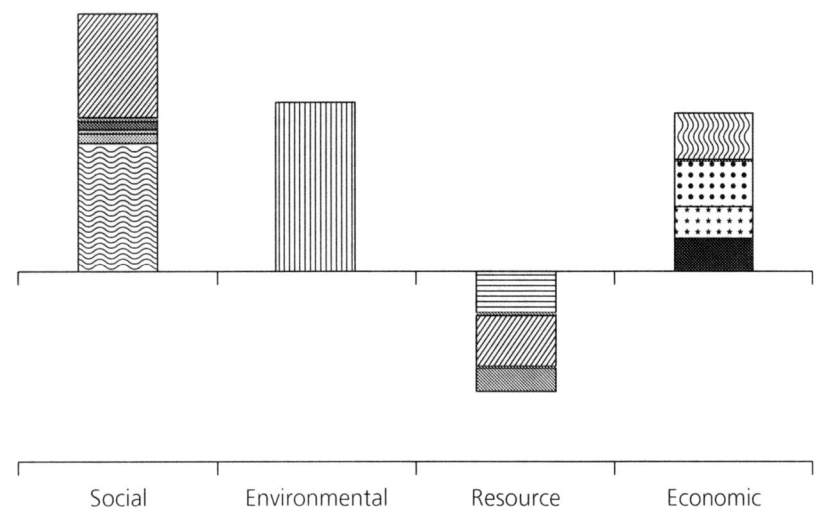

Figure 4.2 Energy from landfill gas SAM signature.

of whether energy is going to be captured from it). Rather, given the 'before' and 'after' comparison which is being undertaken, there is an environmental benefit in this particular case. The SAMi was estimated to be 66% for this signature.

In comparison to a typical oil and gas SAM signature, this signature indicates a higher relative social benefit via the jobs multiplier while having a relatively lower contribution from the value of the product. The latter aspect is easier to explain. In an oil and gas project, products include mobility, heating and pharmaceuticals (derived from petrochemicals). Of these elements, pharmaceuticals (as measured by current prices) have the highest social value. In the case of the landfill gas project, heating is the only product produced and this will have a lower average social value compared to an oil and gas project. Why the jobs multiplier effect is different is not clear but it must reflect the spending patterns of those working on this project, the relative labour intensity compared to an oil and gas field development and the location where the project takes place.

Tree planting project

The final project presented is a tree planting scheme where an indigenous forest (in Scottish terms) is being planted with the expectation that it will be there in perpetuity (the SAM signature for this is presented in Figure 4.3). This signature generates a high SAMi (of 94%) because of the large environmental benefit generated from creating a permanent forest. The two components of the environmental bar in Figure 4.3 are made up of the carbon soaking effect of the forest (in the lower half) and the biodiversity gain from having the forest (in the upper half). What is missing from the signature, however, is any psychic benefit which accrued to individuals who spend time in the forest and leave with an increased sense of well-being. It proved impossible to monetise this element when this SAM was produced and if it were to be considered in a formal project evaluation setting then it could be included as one of the 'bubble' items discussed previously. Further, this project is a good example of how SAM measured performance is a function of the current nature of society. Tree planting provides a huge benefit in an unsustainable society and this is reflected in its relative SAMi. In a sustainable world, however, tree planting may not yield such a positive result.

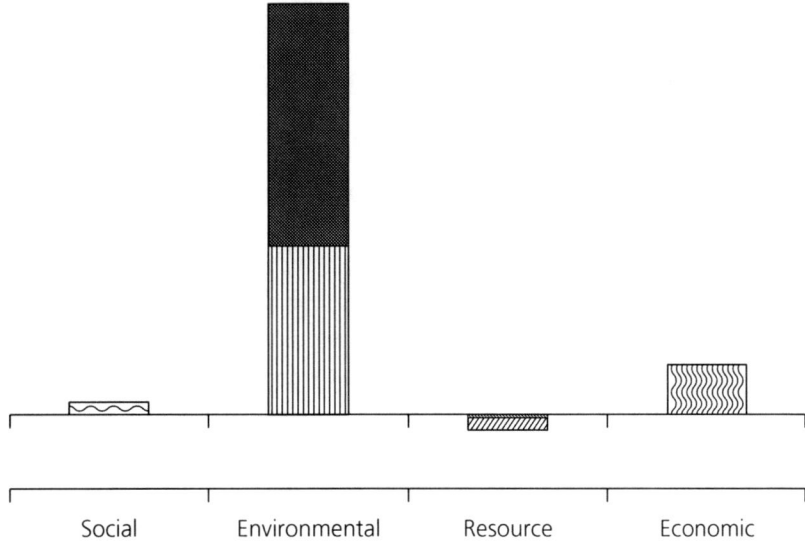

| Social | Environmental | Resource | Economic |

Figure 4.3 Tree planting SAM signature.

Table 4.2: SAMs for different projects

SAM subject matter	Social	Environmental	Resource	Economic	SAMi
	Each element as a percentage of total bar chart area				
Oil and Gas	43.2	−19.0	−17.9	19.9	26.1
Landfill	36.4	23.9	−17.2	22.5	65.6
Tree planting	2.5	84.1	−3.2	10.2	93.6

SAM signatures are, therefore, dependent on the current prices in a particular economy as well as the SD profile of an economy.

By way of comparison, Table 4.2 summarises the data from the three different types of projects on which the SAM was piloted.

This chapter now moves to consider views of the SAM. These views have been gathered from a variety of sources and focus around three main forums: (1) interviews with individuals who are interested in SD evaluation (including those within BP but also from outside of that organisation); (2) feedback obtained from audiences where the SAM has been presented and (3) 'expert' group workshops where social and environmental accountants, and economists were asked to evaluate the SAM.

Evaluating the SAM

The purpose of this part of the book is to start the process of reflecting upon the SAM and seeks to provide information on: the perceived credibility of the SAM (by reference to internal and external audiences), the areas of SAM which make audiences uncomfortable and the overall perceived usefulness of SAM. Observations are organised around four themes: (1) the extent to which the SAM 'works' in simple terms (including discussions about its functionality); (2) concerns about interdependencies and modelling in complex environments; (3) reservations about monetisation and what is presently not in the SAM because it cannot be monetised and (4) issues which would arise from applying the SAM outside of the UK/'developed' world context.

The first pertinent observation to make is that almost without exception meeting participants and interviewees were positive about the need for organisations to develop tools/approaches/methods for reflecting upon SD impacts. In addition, the fact that any tool could only shed light on the impacts, rather than provide a definitive answers, was universally accepted. The observations made about the SAM should, therefore, be viewed in that context.

Functionality

When the SAM was presented to oil and gas audiences, they readily identified the pattern of costs and benefits which the SAM depicts as being accurate (once the point of view of society was taken, rather than the company's point of view). This suggests that the SAM 'makes sense' to those in the industry who are most likely to have a feel for the impacts of oil and gas field development. In addition, one member of an audience to which the SAM was presented noted that the SAM signature is akin to a chemical signature picture and hence is likely to have 'traction' with chemical engineers. While the SAM 'spoke' to oil and gas audiences it was also clear that it presented a picture that had not been seen or thought about before in any depth. One oil and gas interviewee noted that he was 'impressed with the tool, but disturbed by parts of it ... being disturbed says more about me and where I am coming from than the model itself ... for example, that taxation can be a social good, I had not thought of tax in that way before'. Thus the SAM signature presented both known and unknown data and clearly shifted perceptions.

A particular contribution of the SAM that was articulated was that it brought together the various elements of SD, and for many individuals seeing all these elements together was arresting. At one meeting, for example, meeting participants were enthusiastic about the ability of the SAM to communicate the tradeoffs and outcomes from oil and gas field development in concrete terms. It was suggested that where discussions could become polarised about whether or not a development is good or bad, the SAM would provide a way of framing why something would be seen as positive to one person but not to another. It was suggested that the SAM signature made it clear where someone was 'standing in order to judge good and bad'. Thus, it was thought that this could take the 'heat' out of the conflict about whether or not a project was wholly good/bad and enable a discussion about which aspects are good/bad from certain perspectives. Starting such a conversation with a more complete picture was viewed as being valuable.

In a similar vein, the ability to estimate the ratio of damage to benefit which is implicit in the SAM was of interest to those who saw the tool. In particular, the ability to identify the key elements which could be changed in order to enhance a project's SD profile was seen as a valuable characteristic of the SAM. This also suggests that the SAMi is not necessarily the only useful metric that may be drawn from the model. For example, ratios of air pollution externalities to benefits of mobility were of interest (as they point towards the extent to which the price of fuel does not capture external costs and hence price changes which could be anticipated if the polluter pays principle is applied).

At one meeting, participants were keen to know if there was an expected/optimal/anticipated range for the SAMi. The desire to know this arose from meeting participants who saw the SAM as being useful in assessing outcomes (as opposed to those who viewed the SAM as only being useful to raising issues/awareness of SD impacts). Having noted that interest, all meeting participants agreed that the SAM would be more useful as a ranking device than a way of communicating an absolute measure of SD. In addition, ease of use was viewed as being crucial if a tool was to be used at all. One interviewee identified the tradeoff as a question of 'how scientific and how quantitative does the modelling become before it becomes a "black box" which cannot be used or understood by those not specialised in the use of the SAM?'. This interviewee preferred understandability to precision (which in any event, given the complexities of SD, would be spurious precision). As a result, ease of use was preferred to having a more complex and accurate model, if a choice had to be made. Having noted this, a number of meeting participants also expressed concern about issues that may arise if the complexities of the real world were not adequately captured.

Interdependencies and modelling

Two concerns in this area were raised. First, some participants expressed uncertainty about whether or not it was possible to make assessments of social aspects of project impacts because no one knows what a socially sustainable society looks like. This was in contrast to modelling around environmental categories where it was believed that some knowledge of what is sustainable and what is not exists. One individual phrased up a need to have an idea of 'social carrying capacity' before including social aspects in an evaluation framework.

There are two ways such concerns can be addressed. In the first instance, given the SAM is not an account of SD itself (as argued before, it is an account of relative performance in an unsustainable society) then the need to know what a sustainable state looks like does not preclude evaluating the extent to which progress is being made away from an unsustainable state. Further, it could be argued that negative social externalities are an indication of a socially unsustainable society and as such the SAM provides a glimpse of the way in which society is unsustainable. The second way in which this broader concern can be addressed is to argue that existing laws and norms with respect to what behaviour we will tolerate as a society provides an approximation of our current social carrying capacity (this of course begs the question as to whether or not society has actively engaged with what norms are acceptable, to what extent individuals are informed about what these norms are and the role that relative power plays in their formation; these are very complex matters and are beyond the scope of this piece of work, but they remain pertinent). Certainly, in very simplistic terms this is the idea behind using national SD strategies/frameworks to ground the social aspects of the SAM in particular, but also the indicator set of the model as well. In addition, using some national framework also makes SAM potentially transferable to other countries. Just as environmental impacts of pollution varies depending on physical location, so too do social impacts (see also the final element of discussion in this section of the applicability of the SAM outside of the UK).

In addition to uncertainties about how to model social sustainability, the interdependencies between elements of the social world also caused some individuals to have reservations about the directional influence suggested in the SAM. This particular concern played out in using taxation as a linking device between the project and social sustainability and the depiction of this as a positive externality. Specifically it was argued that while taxation does provide social infrastructure via Government spending, a project will itself draw on infrastructure (created by past taxation). For example, an educated workforce is the outcome of tax spent in the past and is available to an organisation to develop their projects. Likewise, past taxation spending has provided and energy and transportation infrastructure which is used in a current project with no direct charge. As a result, it was argued that (at best) there would be a neutral outcome from taxation paid by any one project. There are grounds for accepting this argument, however, it is impossible to know to what extent it is true and what the 'balance of payments' is between current taxation paid and the use of infrastructure. As a result, the taxation element of the SAM remains as it is at present. This point does, however, allude to a more general point of how much complexity can be modelled in such a tool and how much this is likely to matter in an overall evaluation (that is, as with any modelling, materiality has to be considered).

As noted before, the desire in developing the SAM was to create a simple tool that could be understood by those who use it. Further, as far as possible it was hoped that the judgements underlying the SAM are transparent to those who encounter it. As a result, the SAM signature must be treated with an appropriate degree of caution. At the same time, however, where complexity can be modelled and where it impacts the SAM signature it should be undertaken. It seems that the complexity arises in both generic aspects of the model and specific contexts of application. Where the complexity rests with taxation factors and such like (and when and if sufficient work is done to enable determination of, for example, taxation multipliers and/or interdependencies) then these can be 'hard wired' into any model. Before that time, however, the best one can hope for is transparency as to what assumptions have been made.

Reservations about monetisation

As would be expected, a number of individuals expressed reservations about using a money metric to capture aspects of SD which can either not be easily monetised or which should not be monetised on principle. For example, the impact of a project on local cultures (specifically in the developing world, but also in more remote communities within the UK) was given as an example of impacts that could not be usefully monetised. In addition, the quality of the jobs created by a development (for example, the extent to which they would require workers to be away from their families for periods of time) was deemed to be a relevant for evaluating social aspects of a project but again an issue that was difficult to monetise. From an environmental perspective, the loss of critical natural capital and how that could be monetised was also raised as creating a problem for any monetised model. While acknowledging the validity of these points, there are two possible responses to them. First, to develop a way in which such aspects could usefully be considered in SD evaluation (either alone or in conjunction with the SAM). Second, to consider how one could tell if these issues are material and if so, how material are they to SD assessment.

Concerns of a more philosophical nature were also raised. Some argued that nature stands by itself and should not be described in monetary terms. If this is done it could be argued that society legitimates the exploitation of nature. Others would argue that capitalism's reduction of all aspects of life to exchange values is what causes exploitation. Thus, adding more of the same thing (via monetisation) is unlikely to resolve the core reason for exploitation (which are broadly traced to beliefs and systems in the above two arguments). Still others argue that, as an intermediate step, there is value in confronting unsustainability using a language that people understand

and which is currently used to direct behaviour. There is a cogent argument that to refuse to engage on the terms in which organisations currently do business means that voices are not heard at all or, at best, are marginalised. While both 'sides' of the monetisation debate have credibility, the position taken in this report is that monetisation using the language of business is useful for initiating a dialogue which may lead to more fundamental philosophical discussions.

As is evident from the construction of the SAM, one way to deal with aspects which should or could not be monetised is to include these aspects presented alongside the SAM (framed up as having information in bubbles). The use of the word bubbles arose from the idea that these elements would be likely to arise from individuals having their say about critically important aspects: hence 'speech bubbles' would emerge from the process. In addition, this notion is appealing in that it implies a transparency about the issues and avoids constructing 'checklists' of elements which has a much more mechanical feel to it. This does, however, beg the question as to how bubbles are then incorporated into any decision-making process. The only situation where a bubble item was encountered in the SAM modelling reported on here was when a recognisable positive externality (enjoyment from being in a forest) could not be monetised. As such, the SAM provided a conservative picture of SD impact which does not have the same implications as a SAM presenting an overgenerous picture of SD impact and having a significant negative externality in bubble form.

There would appear to be many possible ways to deal with bubbles in a decision-making process. They could be used in some sort of balancing process with the SAM signature. The bubbles could be (by agreement, with or without stakeholders) allocated importance as against percentage points of the SAMi. Alternatively, and again depending on their nature, there could be agreement that some bubbles are always assigned priority over the SAM signature in decisions. This latter approach may be relevant in the case of critical natural capital, for example. Either way, the fact that there is a mechanism for crucial SD elements to be taken into account would be necessary for any monetised tool.

A further issue which emerged in the context of this discussion was the materiality of things that could not be monetised, especially in the context of impacts on local communities and quality of jobs (loss of critical natural capital was viewed as material, full stop). If these impacts are not material then regardless of whether or not they are monetised it may not be necessary to include them in a decision-making heuristic (for example, the quality of jobs in the forest plant-ing scheme is most likely not material). If their severity, as judged by a project team and/or stakeholders, is material then they should be included as bubble items. In this case, materiality is under-defined, a problem which is also emerging in the context of social, environ-mental, SD and/or corporate social reporting decisions (see, for example, AccountAbility, 2003). One interviewee, however, cau-tioned that while identifying material impacts in a concrete manner was useful 'there will always be a bun fight at the end of the day to control what value is assigned' as the stakes are potentially high.

In summary, while there was agreement that monetisation was potentially a problem, there were few suggestions as to how one could challenge the primacy of financial measurement of success without, in some stage of the transition, generating 'alternative' monetary measures. Thus, while conceptually there are clearly issues in monetisation, those who interacted with the SAM could recognise the practical use of experimenting with monetisation. The proviso on doing this, however, was that one should not believe that a straightforward answer could be found using such an approach. In addition, substituting monetisation for groups of people making their preferences and choices explicit was not preferred by anyone: monetisation should not eliminate the need to think about issues.

Non-UK application of the SAM

A number of presentations were made in the UK to individuals who worked in the oil and gas industry in other countries, including lesser developed countries. There were several elements of the SAM which it was felt would change if applied outside of a UK/developed world context. These elements would have implica-tions for the 'results' of the SAM as well as how useful the SAM would be. First (and coming back to an earlier discussion with respect to how the combined impact of projects may be greater than the sum of the parts) it was believed that in economies which were heavily reliant on the extractive industry it may be harder to draw boundaries around individual projects. Given that an entity may have a relative large share of economic activity in any one location, their impact (either direct or through influence) could be substantial. These impacts could also be at odds with the SD agenda. This point has been made by Ross (2001) who examined the economic and social performance of less developed countries with and without extractive sectors. Perhaps surprisingly, countries with extractive sectors (oil and gas as well as minerals/mining) tended to do poorly in terms of poverty because of the disruptive effect of an extractive industry (unless well managed). In particular, countries with extractive sectors tended to suffer from high rates of corruption, authoritarian governments, government ineffectiveness, military spending and civil war with a knock on effect for citizens in such countries. Thus this report suggests that the presence of extractive industries is not always or straightforwardly a 'good thing' for lesser developed countries.

The second area where special considerations may come into play is in linking taxation to social benefit. As previously indicated, this aspect requires an SD strategy in order to identify agreed social aspects of SD. If a country does not have well-defined SD priorities then the linking of taxation to benefits would be harder to determine. In addition, and more crucially, in countries where the government spending is concentrated on funding a war (or on the oppression of parts of the local population) then the likelihood that positive social externalities will arise from taxation is much less. Indeed, in such a context the social impact of taxation spend may in fact be a negative externality. To be intellectually honest, these links would have to be made. It was, however, believed that such a close linking would raise considerable questions and create pressures on the organisation/project which used the SAM (see also Global Witness, 2004, and www.publishwhatyoupay.org).

Finally, where oil and gas is exploited and used in the same country, then all the costs and benefits as reflected in the SAM signature of the activity are found in that country (with the exception of transboundary pollution impacts, the most important of which in this context is greenhouse gases which have a warming effect on a global scale regardless of where they emanate from, although the extent of such impacts depends on location). In contrast, if oil and gas is exploited in one location and transported to another for combustion there is a geographic dispersion of costs and benefits. Economic benefits may be transferred to a holding company country, the cost of resources lost is borne by the developing country while the local pollution impact and social benefit of the product will fall in the country of consumption. The global pollution impact (via greenhouse gas emissions) is likely to affect some parts of the globe regardless of where the benefit of consumption occurs. Equity considerations with respect to this type of distribution are of relevance to SD assessments (especially given the pivotal role of intra-generational equity in SD debates) yet it is not clear how such issues could be played out in a SAM. This is an area which has yet to be fully debated and resolved.

In summary, this section has sought to raise (and to a lesser extent resolve) issues that arise in the application of the SAM. These issues have been raised in a number of public and private arenas where the SAM was presented and debated. Some of the issues could be resolvable with more/better data while other aspects of the concerns will always remain unresolved (objections to monetisation being one of them). The aim of this section was not to dismiss the concerns, but to consider them in more depth and provide such responses that can be offered. At the end of the discussion, it is hoped that the degree to which caution should be exercised around the SAM (and indeed any model purporting to describe SD impacts) is more evident.

Conclusions

To date, this book has introduced the notion of SD and outlined the various ways in which it may be possible to evaluate the extent to which society is moving towards/away from SD and/or the nature of current unsustainability. Of the various approaches, the work focuses on one monetised modelling approach, that of the SAM. The functionality of the SAM has been described in some depth (in Chapter 3) and this chapter has continued that journey by outlining how the SAM has been used within BP. The projects described are real activities which are being undertaken by BP. While the SAM was not used to decide if these projects should be undertaken, it was used on them to develop and test its functionality. In addition to internal sense checking of the SAM, it has also been presented to a large number of individuals in a wide array of settings (including from one-to-one discussions, focus group discussions and to presentations at conferences). From these interactions a series of pressure points could be identified with respect to the design and use of the SAM. These issues have been exercised in this chapter in order to further shed light on the functionality of the SAM.

The first four chapters, therefore, bring us to a turning point in the book with attention now shifting to how other organisations seek to operationalise SD. These discussions were grounded in discussions about how organisations could find ways to measure, manage and target set for SD objectives and the particular role of accounting tools in this process. In the first instance, practices in the oil and gas industry are examined before analysis shifts to other industries, namely construction and electricity generation.

Sustainable Development in Decision Making in the Oil and Gas Industry

Introduction

Until now this book has focused on the activities of one organisation and how it has sought to address sustainable development (SD). In addition, one tool (Sustainability Assessment Model, SAM) has been introduced as a potential way to inform SD performance assessment. This chapter widens the focus from one organisation and one tool to other organisations in the oil and gas industry and the ways in which they seek, if at all, to undertake SD evaluation. The investigation, therefore, sheds light on the wider applicability of the SAM as well as alternative ways of evaluating SD performance. Before this analysis, however, the chapter introduces a sector-wide initiative that purports to address SD.

Sector strategy for SD

The oil and gas industry comprises a large array of organisations which undertake a variety of activities. These activities include exploration, production, refining and retailing as well as service activities that support these core processes. In addition, oil and gas based products permeate our society and support other processes and activities, such as energy production, transportation and chemicals (such as fertilizers and pharmaceuticals). The focus of this research, however, is not on the large array of organisations which are in some way connected to oil and gas products. Rather, the focus is on organisations involved in the exploration and extraction of oil and gas.

Attempts to understand, articulate and address the SD impact by this aspect of the oil and gas industry have been taken by its industry body, the UK Offshore Operators Association Ltd (UKOOA). In particular, UKOOA has produced a sector SD strategy (UKOOA, 2001), against which it has reported progress in subsequent years (UKOOA, 2003, 2004, 2005, 2006). UKOOA's vision for SD is expressed thus:

> We will strive to maintain a competitive industry capable of attracting continued investment and so contribute to economic prosperity through provision of energy, creation of jobs and development of technology, while generating a return for investors. We will value our workforce and local communities, assisting them as far as possible to plan realistically for their futures. We will deliver

Table 5.1: UKOOA SD strategic objectives

Element of SD	Sub-element considered
Economic sustainability	◆ Operational efficiencies through co-operation ◆ Maximising mutual benefit with the supply chain and small/medium enterprises ◆ Developing new technologies ◆ Stimulating business activity
Social sustainability	◆ Workforce conditions and safety ◆ Enhancing recruitment, skills and training ◆ Engagement with society – local communities, schools and users of the sea ◆ Managing future structural change
Protecting the environment	◆ Environmental management ◆ Increasing knowledge and understanding of impacts ◆ Managing environmental impacts
Stewardship – making prudent use of natural resources	◆ Overall impacts ◆ Design for environment ◆ Reducing energy use and waste generated ◆ End of operations legacy

Source: UKOOA, 2001.

continual improvement in our safety and environmental performance while making prudent use of natural resources (UKOOA,
2001, p. 14).

Four areas are focused on within the UKOOA strategy and these are
outlined in Table 5.1.

These high level objectives set in 2001 were underpinned by com-
mitments to undertake certain actions from 2001 until 2003 when
performance against various targets was reported. In addition, data
from various sources was used to provide information on current
and past performance in these areas and a 'roadmap' from 1990 to
2010 was provided to put the strategy into a longer-term context.
This framing has lead to the development of an SD indicator set,
conceptualised in the form of an indicator wheel. Figure 5.1 outlines the current indicator wheel (this was refined in 2005 from the
original wheel) and in each of the nine areas listed there are corres-
ponding indicators (forming a total indicator set of 22 items). See
http://www.oilandgas.org.uk/issues/sustainability/introduction.htm
for more information.

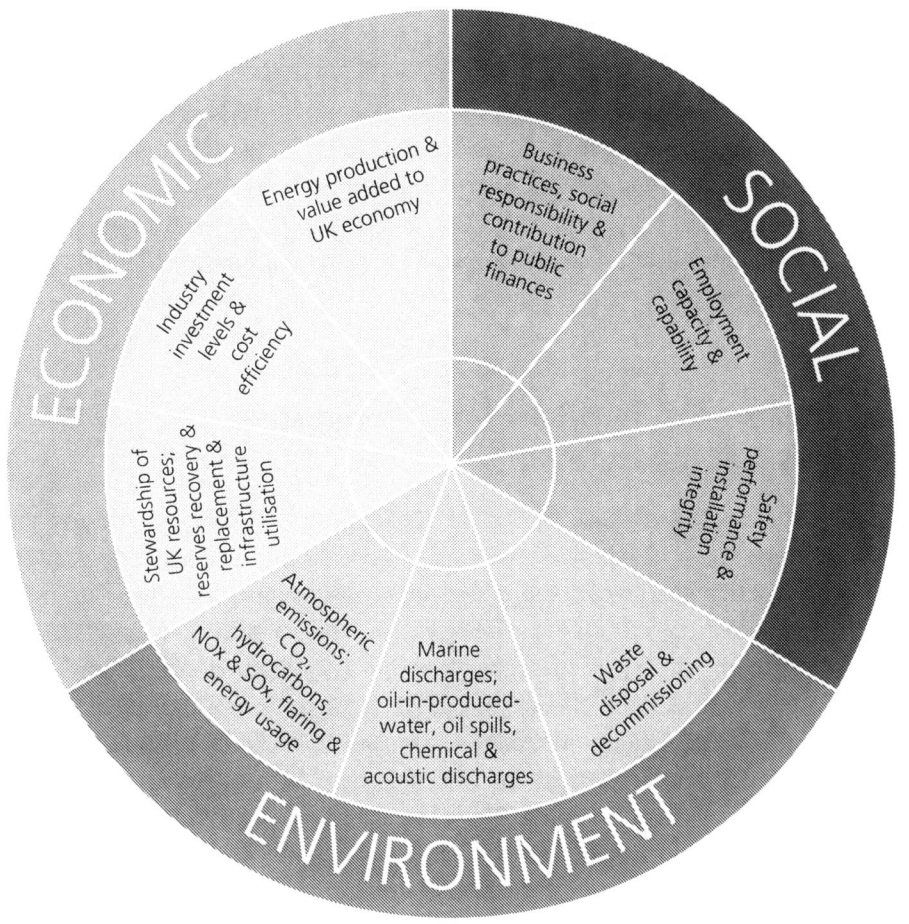

Figure 5.1 The SD indicator wheel (UKOOA, 2005).

The UKOOA work, in the parlance used in Chapter 2, takes an indicators set approach to measuring, managing and target setting for SD. The approach has involved industry participants as well as stakeholders in the industry (see UKOOA, 2003, p. 74). These stakeholders included individuals representing Government/ Government Advisors (for example, the Department of Trade and Industry, Department for Environment and Rural Affairs, the Sustainable Development Commission and the Scottish Executive), local or regional representatives (for example, local Chambers of Commerce, City and Regional Councils), sustainability, environment and social organisations (such as WWF, Marine Conservation, Earthwatch and the Global Reporting Initiative) and others (namely academics and representatives of the socially responsible/ethical investment movement).

Given the processes described above, one could argue that participants in the offshore oil and gas industry in the UK are likely to be informed about SD issues and to have a framework within which to place their company activities. It is to the interviewees perceptions of SD (and approaches to performance assessment) that attention now turns.

SD evaluation in oil and gas companies (individual interviews)

As is evident from the above section, the UK offshore oil and gas industry has started thinking about its SD impacts, how these impacts can be controlled and how performance may be communicated to outside parties. This suggests that organisations within the industry will have had exposure to the language of SD and may have considered the role of their organisations in contributing to SD. Indeed, many member companies of UKOOA are longstanding social, environmental or SD reporters in stand-alone corporate reports (with Shell and BP perhaps being the best known of these in the UK, but noting that a number of other UKOOA members produce non-financial reports: for example, Agip/ENI (since 1996), Amerada Hess (since 1996), Enterprise Oil (since 1995), Exxon Mobil, USA (since 1999) and Total (since 2002)).

It was with UKOOA member organisations that interviews for this project were sought. In total interviews were conducted with thirteen individuals within five oil and gas companies through seven separate interviews. Interviewees included those with responsibility for overall management of organisations' operations as well as those with health/safety/environment/SD responsibilities. In all but one of the interviews two interviewees were present. The interviews were not taped, but extensive notes were taken during the interview and interview summaries were created and used as the basis for analysis. In addition to these 'core' oil and gas interviews, two additional interviews were undertaken which supplemented understanding of the oil and gas industry interviews. The first of these was with a supplier to the offshore industry which itself had paid considerable attention to SD issues. The second additional interview was undertaken with an individual working for an oil and gas regulator body. The following, therefore, represents the views of those most likely to be considering SD performance assessment and hence most likely to have thought about the issues that are involved in this type of activity.

Three elements are developed from the interviews. First, how each organisation undertakes project evaluation is described and linked to SD evaluation. Second, the way in which each organisation attempts to take account of SD (within the context of corporate social responsibility, CSR) is outlined. This information, in combination with how project evaluation is undertaken, thus provides insight into the possibilities for SD assessment within the organisations interviewed. Finally, an attempt is made to ascertain influences on how organisations consider SD performance evaluation.

Project evaluation approaches

All organisations interviewed had formal processes for the evaluation of project opportunities. The degree of formality, however, varied among the interviewees. In the main, the more formalised the approaches were, the more standardised they were as well. At the same time, the place of SD evaluation within project appraisal systems was also identified and linked to the general approach adopted. Table 5.2 provides an indication of the range of approaches which were evident (noting that these descriptions are of generalised approaches rather than descriptions of any one organisation's approach).

In all cases where formal project evaluation was undertaken, procedures incorporated the following two interlinked features. First, a multi-stage evaluation approach was undertaken with each subsequent stage incorporating more detail than the last. Second, some form of external (in terms of external to the project team) overview of the project appraisal process took place at what were deemed to be 'critical' stages of project evaluation.

This second aspect introduces the possibility for someone external to the project team (but internal to the organisation and who may, for example, have responsibility for SD) injecting SD evaluation

Table 5.2: Approaches to project appraisal approach and incorporation of SD

Characterisation of process

♦ Goals very formally stated with detailed standardised approaches to achieving ends.
♦ Strongly driven by a strategic vision which percolates down to detailed operational processes and procedures.
♦ SD goals formally stated, measured and monitored.

♦ Goals formally stated but with high level of choice as to how the stated ends are achieved.
♦ Does not appear to be highly top down in terms of design, but may produce this effect nevertheless due to formality of goal formulation and monitoring processes.
♦ Some SD evaluation takes place but no standardisation of approaches and hence no depth of experience in the organisation.

♦ Goals formally stated and relatively standardised approaches to decision making.
♦ No SD decision-making approaches made explicit so little work undertaken.

♦ Comparatively unspecified decision-making procedures.
♦ At the same time, strong top-down specification of what counts as success for the organisation.
♦ No overt SD decision making in place but an assumption that should it be value relevant it would be undertaken spontaneously.

into project appraisal. Likewise, if project 'gatekeepers' have SD knowledge it may be possible that, in the absence of a formal SD screen, aspects of SD are considered during project appraisal. Indeed, one interviewee spoke of 'informal norms' developing from gate-keeping activities (albeit that these norms did not currently include aspects of SD). Thus, if gatekeepers consistently ask certain questions about SD and/or reject projects until they address SD then project appraisal could evolve to include these considerations without formal specification by the organisation.

One other point is relevant to note at this stage. Given that oil and gas projects are invariably joint ventures involving several organisations, project appraisal routines usually involve partners in a project. When a company is the operator of the project, they use their own project appraisal routines. There are also, however, meetings with all partners and, as a result, at critical decision points the consent of all the partners has to be obtained. This offers opportunities for SD evaluation to be more widely adopted (for example, if an operator includes such evaluation and convinces the partners that this is a good idea) as well as dangers that there will be reversion to the lowest common denominator with respect to SD understanding and prioritisation. In the particular case of the oil and gas industry this may also encourage industry norms of behaviour to develop over time. This point should not, however, be overstated. There are significant differences between industry companies, perhaps most notably on their attitudes to environmental issues as evidenced by their response to climate change.

While project appraisal approaches were centred on financial aspects (using conventional evaluation methods), all approaches also incorporated additional forms of analysis. Most frequently these included health and safety as well as environmental evaluations (for example, at a minimum whether or not project design would allow regulatory requirements to be met). In addition, for projects of a critical size/impact socio-economic evaluations would be undertaken. While organisations themselves were interested in non-financial aspects of performance, interviewees noted that regulators and other stakeholders were also interested in these aspects.

As a result, SD evaluation of a sort could be argued to be taking place within this industry. In most instances, however, this is taking place without being explicitly recognised as SD evaluation. In particular, aspects of the SD agenda such as social impacts (jobs and health/safety considerations), economic impacts of decisions (for communities, suppliers and other users of space, such as fishermen) and potential environmental impacts (including biodiversity and the pollution impact of extraction, but not of subsequent combustion) are taken into account in project appraisal. As one interviewee put it, there are 'metrics for safety performance, environmental performance and business performance – these are systematically derived, measurements taken and reporting against these types of headings' takes place.

What is important in the context of this work, however, is that it is relatively rare for all these aspects to be combined together in some self-reflective form of SD evaluation. It is even rarer for such an evaluation to take the viewpoint of how society is affected by a project. Rather, the norm is that evaluations take the organisation's perspective in assessing impacts. Likewise, questions of the appropriateness of the scale of impacts (for example, if the carrying capacity of the environment is compromised) did not appear to be addressed by any interviewee organisations.

Drawing from the above observations it is possible to suggest that there are opportunities within current approaches to project evaluation to incorporate SD assessments. In many instances aspects of SD performance are incorporated into project appraisal. Consideration of aspects of SD, however, does not constitute SD evaluation as such and this was emphasised in one interview as supporting their organisation's decision not to develop a standardised approach to SD. In particular, this interviewee noted that if a standardised approach (such as the SAM) were used:

> the worry is ... that people would think that you can trade off all the elements presented in the four capitals. In that case, you create the 'wrong mental place' for people to start from ... [our view] of the right way to do this is to sit around the table and pull out the issues (social, environmental and economic) from the [company] and external perspective. When you have it all on the table you can get better judgements and decisions. You would quantify it all if you can but there will always be qualitative issues and you shouldn't run away from these. Managers are skilled at doing this task and knowing intuitively about risk etc ... SD is about integrative, holistic thinking, not crude tradeoffs. Judgements will always affect the elements [in SD evaluation] but once it is quantified you don't want people to give up thinking about the issues.

Further, if standardised approaches to project appraisal are followed then SD has to be part of the standard package if it is to have traction in an organisation. There was evidence, however, of various layers for formality for the recognition, and hence widespread use, of various tools including: informal recommendation by a gatekeeper for its use, repeated use of a tool (and hence its usefulness would be inferred by others seeking appropriate tools) to being peer reviewed and included in the mandatory set of tools for project appraisal. One interviewee expressed it thus: 'if something is not in the "bible" [the project appraisal protocols] it is invisible'. In contrast, if project appraisal approaches allow leeway for inclusion of non-standard evaluations then some organisational mechanism would be required to create the possibility for SD to be incorporated into the decision process (perhaps via SD training/awareness/literacy which would ensure that all project members would consider SD in the normal course of their activities).

In summary, it is possible to suggest that despite an industry-wide strategy for SD, and despite organisations suggesting that they consider SD, there is little formal evaluation of SD taking place at the point in time when projects are sanctioned. This suggests that if there is SD thinking taking place in the organisation it has yet, in all instances, to percolate through to operational levels. This does not, however, mean that no consideration of SD is taking place within the organisations interviewed. The next section draws out from the interviews how organisations are considering SD outside of their project appraisal routines.

Organisational approaches to CSR

All interviewees stressed that the way in which SD may be thought of in relation to project appraisal was conditioned by their organisation's approach to CSR in general. The implicit assumption behind these statements is that CSR is the overarching concern within which SD concerns can be articulated. This nesting of SD within CSR may limit the extent to which organisations think about SD aspects beyond those which can be articulated within a business case. Given SD is primarily a spatial notion (rather than an organisational concept), considering SD from the perspective of the entity may also constrain corporations' ability to effectively tackle SD challenges within their sphere of control. Leaving aside these limitations, insight into how CSR is tackled by organisations (and links, if any, to SD) emerged from the interview process.

As with project appraisal, approaches to CSR differed within interviewee organisations as well as differing over time in the same organisation. A top-down approach which focused on the strategic importance of CSR, however, appeared to be the norm. For one interviewee the 'tone from the top' was important in the battle for 'winning hearts of minds' for CSR/SD to be seriously considered within the organisation. For another interviewee the tone from the top for SD specifically (and to a lesser degree CSR) was itself lacking and this, combined with a very command and control culture within the organisation, resulted in this particular manager facing limited possibilities for addressing SD. Specifically this arose from 'a lack of resources [and] little flexibility to have something not sanctioned by [head office]' and the need to be 'where the corporation is at'. A similar story emerged from another interviewee who noted that their organisation 'has a very very top down approach to things … it is not at all a collegiate organisation … it is very very directive, especially the boss man'. In this case the 'boss man' was resistant to ideas of SD and, to a lesser degree, CSR. As a result, aspects of these agendas were not addressed in this organisation.

For some organisations, a strategic focus on SD (specifically, rather than on CSR) changed over time with interest in SD waning at the present time. For this organisation, however, CSR remained an ongoing focus, albeit that elements of CSR change over time. Another interviewee noted that while an SD position was not formally articulated, to the extent that SD would be considered it would first be articulated within their CSR report. Further, this interviewee noted that this report 'reflects a longstanding stream of activities … which [now] has a new name'. Likewise, another interviewee observed that when they started to think about SD they took a stand-alone report (perceived to represent good SD reporting practice) from an industry peer and mapped what they did against what was in the report. With the exception of two items this interviewee asserted that their organisation was doing the same things as the reporter but without labelling these actions as being related to SD.

The above observations raise the possibility that the use of the term SD in external reporting may not necessarily signal a substantively new focus on this area. Rather, it could be that existing activities are merely being renamed as being SD (one interviewee stated at the start of their interview that 'the first thing to note is that in talking about the agenda we use SD and CSR interchangeably'). This would suggest that one might not see a link between reporting and evaluation activities for SD because the reporting does not reflect a fundamentally changed focus within the organisation.

Noting the above, the question then becomes how a high-level desire to think about SD (perhaps under the banner of CSR) is reflected within organisation routines and the link (if any) between these routines and project appraisal. Several interviewees saw problems with making this link. For example, one noted that SD had proven to be 'hard to apply to business planning processes … because extra issues arise when you move beyond the project level. An organisation is greater than the sum of its projects'. Likewise, the rolling out of SD implications from strategic to operational levels was not viewed as being straightforward.

In other instances it was noted that the CSR routines within the organisation were decoupled from project appraisal. For example, for one organisation project appraisal and selection processes focused narrowly on capital stewardship with CSR strands not being taken into account in that process. One interviewee expressed the mis-match thus: 'the combination of activities are shared with wider external audiences ... these [CSR] reports are not helpful [for project appraisal] and do not grow out of business plans ... business plans are created via the activities of project leaders and managers'.

In summary, from the majority of the interviews it would appear to be unwise to infer that an organisation would have an operational focus on SD from statements about SD in their stand-alone non-financial reporting, if this exists. While both activities may have a common starting point in top management flagging the importance of SD, the two routines (reporting and project evaluation) appear to be largely decoupled in the organisations interviewed for this project.

In contrast, interviews with a more recent reporter seemed to suggest that reporting and activities were not entirely divorced from each other. For this organisation undertaking reporting was viewed internally as a big, and potentially risky, step. In this situation, in order to make sure that there was a comfort with reporting a considerable amount of work was undertaken into examining what was happening within the organisation. There was a perceived need to check that if there was a desire to report on something that there were data systems that would allow reporting to take place. In this case, however, there was again no formally identified link between the two sets of routines (reporting and managing/decision making).

Thus, it can be suggested that where industry and company understanding of SD is still in a relatively early stage, considering SD probably results in the creation of reporting and assessment routines at more or less the same time. For those industry participants who have taken a little longer to consider SD reporting, a more formal linking of reporting and appraisal is possible, albeit that for these interviewees no one had currently fully linked the two.

One interviewee offered some thoughts on how, if at all, the linking between a strategic vision for CSR/SD and operational routines could be achieved:

> the traditional approach is to introduce concepts/ideas and then cascade it through the organisation ... the cascade effect always peters out somewhere. In the introduction phase, therefore, you have to pick key people to influence change. These people are of two sorts: critical for embedding things in the organisation and enthusiasts (people who are opinion formers, enthusiastic and high fliers). The first people who are critical for the embedding work are: auditors, those involved in business improvement routines, business strategy and planning people, stakeholder engagement people, speech writers and peer review/business review people. Using these people to effect change leverages time and creates a snowball effect.

Another interviewee described the process within their organisation thus:

> where there has been more of a bottom-up approach to SD you almost have to by-pass the formal systems in order to get SD used ... the organisation's high level aspirations didn't translate down to each and every project ... different project teams interpreted these [high level aspirations] differently or paid different levels of attention to these ideas/aspirations ... [organisational SD champions] are driven and have the will to embed these things [and in this way] people are moving towards incorporating SD.

In summary, how CSR is considered by the organisations interviewed suggests that CSR routines are unlikely (in the short term at least) to lead to SD considerations finding their way in project appraisal. In particular, CSR routines and project appraisal routines appear not to dovetail with each other. This limits the ability of one set of routines to influence the other.

Influences on approaches to SD evaluation

In this section, other possible influences on approaches to SD evaluation are tentatively developed. The reason for the tentative nature of these findings is that a relatively small percentage of the oil and gas industry were represented in these interviews. While keeping this limitation in mind, several possible influences are posited: (1) head office location and CEO attitudes to SD, (2) the type of operating assets which are managed by the organisation in question and (3) the way in which organisations are influenced by stakeholders. These three factors are interlinked with respect to their impact on SD evaluation.

The head office location of the organisation in question was viewed by interviewees as influencing SD orientation in two ways. First, and as discussed previously, head office preferences with respect to CSR and the use of the language of SD appeared to affect the extent to which SD is considered in subsidiaries. Second, the political environment in different locations may dictate different responses in order to maintain organisational legitimacy with various stakeholders.

The distinction between head quarter locations was framed up around a US focus and a European focus. While it is a crude distinction, it was believed that the 'agenda is different' between these two regions. (See Kolk and Levy, 2001 who found that such a distinction, while crude, 'worked'. See also Kolk, 2005 who found distinctly different trends in environmental reporting between US, Japanese and European corporations. This data supports a difference in approach emerging from head quarter locations.) One interviewee expressed their personal belief that a 'corporate citizenship report is probably as much as you can expect from a US company, head quartered in Dallas with relatively limited European operations'. Another stated that 'if you don't have high levels of activity in Europe it is my impression that you don't have to use the "SD" descriptor for these activities'. A further interviewee suggested that 'the external drivers are different between the USA and the UK, Europe tends to see SD and CSR differently' and, further, that the 'criticism [of SD] at the USA HQ is that you can't talk about SD because the extractive industry is an unsustainable industry. The short-term response is that you have to look, therefore, at corporate responsibility rather than SD'.

Country differences, in combination with different organisational cultures, led one interviewee to state that 'the approach of a corporate is largely dictated by the social and political situation where the company is head quartered and how the organisation seeks to operate'. One pivotal element in how organisations seek to operate appeared to be what they viewed their business to be.

Two interviewees noted that there is an important psychological difference between being an 'oil and gas firm and being an energy firm, with hydrocarbons being one' way to satisfy energy demand. An energy company would, it was suggested, have more comfort with SD language and BP and Shell were offered as examples of industry participants who had started to make this transition.

The nature of the assets operated by a company in particular locations was also suggested to be an important influence on SD awareness. One interviewee linked their 'SD-lite' position to the fact that they are not well known in the street because their company name is not a brand name on forecourts. As a result they are not as visible to consumer stakeholders and hence do not need to formally address SD with that audience. This was in marked contrast to some other organisations in the sector that have a substantial public face.

Even within extraction itself, the type of operations were seen to affect SD orientation. One interviewee made the distinction between large developments and more incremental projects (involving tie backs, for example). Given that more recent North Sea developments have not been large, long-term assets there was an implication that if SD evaluation is taking place it may be outside of the UK context (for example, in the developing world oil and gas fields). Indeed, one interviewee suggested that some developing world countries are perceived to expose you to the need to be more pro-active in SD terms. As they put it 'in a country where 90% of government revenue comes from oil there are lots of issues'.

The final element of the mix with respect to aspects that were thought to influence SD orientation relates to the way in which stakeholders may affect an organisation's propensity to address SD. As has already been outlined, the degree to which an organisation feels it is in the public eye and/or the need to influence consumers was posited as one element in responsiveness to SD. Two other influences were also identified by interviewees: the regulator and UKOOA itself.

One interviewee stated that:

> In practical terms, if the regulator asked for SD related information we would have to measure what they wanted … once you are doing that then you naturally seek to use that information in some

way. If something is being measured it will make its way into management information and it should be possible to derive economic value from having measured and managed something. Thus a requirement from the regulator would eventually lead to a change in performance.

It is unlikely that this situation will come to pass. It was noted that while there is a general policy 'ambiance' within the UK for SD this does not cascade down (to use the metaphor that was used by an oil and gas company interviewee) to the detailed process of regulating. Regulators appeared to be unwilling to 'widen the boundary of debate about SD' because to do so would 'dilute ... power to influence behaviour' because those over who control is sought cannot realistically be held responsible for downstream impacts. Indeed, focusing on, say, the environmental impacts of combusting oil and gas for transportation was viewed as a way of 'letting the oil companies off the hook because you end up talking about what they can't affect so you can't make them accountable'. In the short term, therefore, there was no sense in which the current regulators within the industry would be able to or would wish to bring an SD lens to bear in their regulatory process.

More influence, however, was ascribed to UKOOA in the context of getting SD awareness within oil and gas industry participants (the UKOOA sector strategy was seen to have an effect on some interviewees, while other interviewees were, as one might expect, pivotal to shaping the strategy). The influence of the strategy was specifically noted by one interviewee who stated that: 'SD first came to be thought about within [company name] via the UKOOA sectoral strategy project ... [and] without the UKOOA initiative ... [we] would not be where we are now ... SD is accepted within the organisation as something to consider because of UKOOA's actions.' Having found evidence of the UKOOA work influencing interviewee organisations, it was noted that their 'indicators for SD are useful for the industry, rather than being useful for a specific company. There is a need to balance the UKOOA position/focus, the corporate office position and the local ... activities ... these three elements need to be in harmony'.

Finally, one other organisation stated that they seek to tailor information to the market where the majority of share trades are conducted. For this organisation the majority of trades were in North America and 'issues of civil tort arose which dictated the type of report which was produced'. This aspect further inhibits the deduction of a straightforward link between reporting styles and what may be assumed about internal decision-making processes. It does, however, loosely support the idea that head office location is a factor in propensity to address SD issues.

To conclude, this section has sought to document the extent to which other participants in the oil and gas industry address SD and individual interviewee perceptions of SD evaluation. A minority of those interviewed worked within organisations with some form of explicit SD evaluation, although elements of SD (such as health and safety and environmental impact) are addressed within all interviewee organisations. It also should be noted that those who accepted the request for interview are likely to be among the more aware with respect to SD. This does not bode well for widespread adoption of an SD focus in strategic or operational processes. In order to explore what form evaluations may take, views on the subject from a variety of industry participants were sought.

SD evaluation in oil and gas companies (conference summary)

The final element of this chapter draws from data gathered at a conference run for the oil and gas industry on 'Measuring, managing and target setting for sustainable development: industry, company and project level assessment'. The conference involved presentations on various SD evaluation approaches (including the SAM) followed by break-out workshops. During the workshops that participants were asked their views on performance measurement for SD as well as the desirability of tools for such measurement and evaluation and, as a result, the workshops provide insights into the issues this research is concerned with. Once again it is important to stress that these views are drawn from individuals who are interested in SD and hence will not be reflective of the industry generally (these views are most probably more optimistic than would be the norm). There were some 40 participants in the workshops.

Conference participants were unanimous in their belief that organisations should be measuring SD performance with the majority wishing to see the use of some common approach throughout the oil and gas industry, in order to aid comparison and benchmarking. Having noted that they personally had enthusiasm for SD evaluation, workshop participants were less certain that this could be achieved within their organisations. Indeed, when asked about whether or not companies will report on their social and environmental impacts of their activities within the next 10 years only 36% of the workshop participants saw this happening (in contrast with 97% of this group who believed that companies should do so). Given reporting on SD may trigger (and be triggered by) consideration of SD performance assessment this finding seems to suggest that widespread evaluation of SD is unlikely to happen in the medium term if business continues 'as usual'.

Impediments for SD evaluation were also explored with this group and Table 5.3 summarises the responses obtained (participants were asked to indicate all those items that were applicable from a list of items with space for them to add their own items. On average 3–4 items were chosen). As is evident from the table, there was no

Table 5.3: Factors preventing your organisation from improving its SD target setting, measurement and reporting

Factor	Number indicating is a factor	Percentage of total
No business case	16	12
Short-term focus	16	12
Lack of understanding of issues	16	12
Lack of leadership in this area	15	11
Lack of supportive company culture	15	11
No suitable tools	10	7
The current economic system does not encourage this activity	9	7
Apathy	8	6
Not on the corporate agenda	8	6
Different corporate versus personal values	6	4
No vision for SD	5	4
Too difficult	5	4
Stakeholders do not encourage	2	1
Employees do not pursue	2	1
Legislation prevents such an approach	1	1
	134	99

strong consensus around which factors were responsible for the lack of SD performance reporting. Rather, it would appear that there is a constellation of factors that prevent progress on this front. These factors could be grouped around lack of direct business drivers for evaluation (no business case, short-term focus) and lack of organisational desire to address SD (apathy, not on agenda, lack of leadership, lack of supportive culture, no vision for SD). The former set of reasons accounts for some 25% of the responses while the latter accounts for 38%. This suggests that while the external environment is not supportive of SD, it is organisational factors that are more important for explaining a lack of action in this area. In contrast, lack of understanding in this area and having no suitable tools for SD evaluation accounted for 19% of the factors listed. In combination these findings suggest that there is a considerable amount of work to be done in educating and encouraging organisations to develop practice in this area. Further, it also suggests that without some external pressure to address SD evaluation, such accounting is unlikely to emerge of its own accord.

This same group also had clear ideas about the desirable characteristics of SD evaluation tools. Each participant was asked to indicate the five most important characteristics of SD evaluation tools and Table 5.4 captures the preferences expressed (after quantitative the number of 'votes' tails off sharply).

While there are always dangers with 'wish lists' of desirable attributes, it would appear from the feedback elicited that there are preferences for whole life evaluation approaches. In addition, it would appear that the ability to communicate the results of SD evaluation

Table 5.4: Desirable characteristics of SD evaluation tools

Characteristics	Number of participants indicating this is important (n = 40)
Full life cycle	27
Practical	26
Flexible	23
Qualitative	21
Simple	20
Holistic	16
Quantitative	13

with those working at all levels within the organisation is important. It is, however, worth noting that tensions exist between tools that are practical/flexible/simple and those that have characteristics of full life cycle/holistic.

The final aspect that was investigated in the conference workshop setting was the extent to which SD evaluation was likely to develop in the future. Participants indicated that currently their organisations were not undertaking a great deal of activity in the area of SD performance evaluation (while noting that four participants indicated that their organisations were doing 'a lot' of 'full reporting' of SD performance). The majority of participants anticipated that in 5 years time that this pattern would have changed. As a result, there was an expectation that this area will develop in the medium term.

Conclusions

The purpose of this chapter was to examine how organisations other than BP were approaching SD performance evaluation. As is apparent, there is a framework in the form of the UKOOA sector strategy that provides a context within which participants in this industry could consider issues that SD raises for their organisations. This strategy was noted as being instrumental for some organisations to start the process of thinking about SD. For others, the strategy reflects the range of activities that they are already involved in. While the strategy contains indicators related to SD, it does not develop any assessment methodology that seeks to compare the indicators to existing measures of performance nor integrate the indicators into an overall assessment. It was noted by one interviewee that the moving from an indicators focus towards some combined evaluation of SD for the industry could emerge from the UKOOA work. At the same time, however, such an aspiration was acknowledged to be unrealistic because of the tensions between various members of UKOOA that means that the strategy and associated work have to take all industry participants with it. As a result, while the UKOOA work is undoubtedly helpful in raising the profile of SD in this industry it is unlikely to drive SD performance assessment.

The picture emerging from the interview data is complex. In all interview organisations it was clear that some individuals understood SD, its importance in the public policy agenda as well as the issues that arise for the oil and gas industry. In all cases, however, there appeared to be a disjuncture between putative CSR orientated reporting activities, business management processes and project evaluation. Any SD evaluation that is taking place, therefore, appears to rely on individual passion and small-scale experiments in SD evaluation (such as the SAM) rather than on a programme of evaluation rolled out across the organisation (although it is relevant to note that some interviewees had aspirations in this direction).

Some specific impediments to the spread of SD assessment were identified by interviewees. These included little focus or explicit demand for such assessment from powerful stakeholders within or outside of the organisation coupled with a relative lack of depth of understanding among all stakeholder groups. In addition, a lack of well-proven metrics, models or toolkits for SD evaluation hampered the ability of champions to demonstrate what evaluation would look like and what benefits would flow from it (albeit that this was a less important barrier). In addition, there was a set of structural impediments to SD evaluation, most importantly short termism within the industry and the narrow focus of existing evaluation techniques. Finally, there appears to be a variety of specific factors that influence propensity to develop and use SD evaluation techniques. Of key importance in this area was head office location, the conception of what kind of business one is in (oil and gas versus energy) and the type of assets held.

Taken together, the outlook for SD evaluation in the oil and gas industry is not good in the short term. This begs the question of what is happening in other industries, what lessons may be drawn from them and it is to this question that the book turns. A widening of focus to other industries may also shed light on whether or not the particular constellation of factors in the oil and gas industry that encourage and/or inhibit SD evaluation are found in other sectors.

Sustainable Development Evaluation Outside of the Oil and Gas Industry

Introduction

While the Sustainability Assessment Model (SAM) was developed in the context of the oil and gas industry, there is no reason to assume that it could not be applied in other contexts (with appropriate modification). Indeed, Landcare Research (New Zealand) Ltd have developed the SAM for application in a variety of contexts including: buildings, waste disposal and transportation options (see http://www.landcareresearch.co.nz/research/sustain_business/#frst for more information) and also Bebbington and MacGregor (2003) who outline how the SAM principles could be applied to a construction project. This chapter, therefore, explores the potential for the SAM specifically, and sustainable development (SD) evaluation generally, to be applied outside of the oil and gas sector. Two other industries were considered in this context: the construction and electricity generation sectors. These sectors were chosen for several reasons. First, both industries (like the oil and gas sector) have a role in the play in the development of core services to the economy (built infrastructure and energy respectively). As a result, if these sectors operated in accordance with the principles of SD then an economy would transform significantly. Second, in both sectors there is evidence that SD has been considered by individual firms and by the industry more broadly in the form of statements of strategic intent. Third, both industries could be seen to be project based, like oil and gas. Further, electricity generation, for example, is an industry where (at least ostensibly) the choice of technology is within the direct control of organisations in that industry. In contrast, the construction industry presents a more complex environment within which to seek to achieve SD because more organisations are involved in the provision of built environment and the construction industry is merely one element in this process. As a result, it was hoped that an exploration of SD in the context of these two industries would create insights into the possibilities for more widespread take-up of SD assessment.

As will become apparent, the relative focus on each sector is different with construction having a more in-depth focus than electricity. Initially it was planned to have an equal focus on these two industries. It became apparent, however, that concurrent with this research being conducted the electricity sector was undergoing a series of structural changes resulted in potential interviewees being unable to participate in this research in any breadth or depth. As a result, the chapter will commence with an examination of the insights that were able to be developed from interactions with the construction industry. At the end of the chapter, the interactions with the energy sector will be briefly outlined before some concluding comments are made.

Construction

Two methods were used to develop an understanding of the possibilities for SD assessment in the construction industry. First, interviews with five members of the industry drawn from four organisations were undertaken. The focus of these interviews was on the extent to which construction companies were addressing SD and the problems that were being encountered in that process. The interviews did not delve in great depth into the issue of measuring for SD. The interviewees, however, did touch on this subject from time to time. Second, a workshop with 10 members of the industry was conducted to explore measuring, managing and target setting for SD. This second element was similar in nature and focus to the conference/workshop undertaken with participants from the oil and gas industry in that several possible assessment methods were presented to participants during the workshop and then a discussion of the desirability and feasibility of the various approaches were reviewed as well as the possibilities for SD assessment in general.

In a similar manner to the oil and gas industry, there are industry-wide attempts to articulate how the SD agenda interacts with construction. Table 6.1 outlines two key SD initiatives, but see also CIRIA (2001), Cox et al. (2002) and Upstream (2003) for examples of work in this area (see also http://www.lsx.org.uk/programmes/lscp_page1213.aspx for information on the London Sustainable Construction Initiative and http://www.ciria.org/suds/ for information on sustainable urban drainage systems).

From a rudimental investigation into what is happening with respect to SD in construction, it becomes apparent that there is a myriad of organisations involved in this area. Interviewees indicated that this pattern arises from the nature of construction and has two sources: the extent to which the built environment creates and context for other activities and the complex interrelationships between aspects of construction.

Table 6.1: Key SD-related initiatives on construction/built environment

Initiative	Details and/or further information sources
UK Government work on sustainable construction	There is a long history of work undertaken at the UK Government level with information on current work being located at the following link: http://www.dti.gov.uk/sectors/construction/sustainability/page13691.html. There are three areas of current activity: the sustainable buildings task group, a review and consultation for the Sustainable Construction Strategy (see below) and a consultation paper on proposals for introducing a code for sustainable homes (which is itself issued by the Office of the Deputy Prime Minister).
Building a better quality of life – a strategy for more sustainable construction (Department for Environment, Transport and the Regions, 2000)	This was the first strategy document and included several themes for action: re-use of existing built assets, design for minimum waste, aim for lean construction, minimise energy in construction, minimise energy in building use, avoid polluting the environment, preserve and enhance bio-diversity, conserve water resources, respect people and their local environment, and set targets (benchmarks and performance indicators). Consultation on the updating of this strategy closed in late April 2006.

In the first instance, construction impinges on many aspects of commercial and domestic life in the UK and elsewhere. Likewise, infrastructure for energy and transportation is largely derived from and create patterns of built environments (with their attendant social, environmental and economics impacts). For example carbon dioxide emissions by end users in the UK a good basis from which to demonstrate this point (all data are drawn from http://www.defra.gov.uk/environment/statistics/globatmos/kf/gakf07.htm). The significance of the built environment can be gauged by the fact that in 1970, 41% of carbon dioxide emissions were sourced from transport (12%) and domestic (29%) sources. By 2003, 57% of carbon dioxide emissions arise from transport (29%) and domestic (28%) sources. Taken together it thus becomes apparent how important the shape of the built environment is in driving greenhouse gas emission levels. Further, Casella et al. (2002, p. 5) note that the 'construction industry is a significant part of any economy' and, quoting 2001 figures, that the 'industry employed 1.5 million people in 180,000 companies with a turnover of about 10 per cent of gross domestic product'. Table 6.2 further demonstrates the social and environmental outcomes of the

Table 6.2: Social and environmental impacts emerging in the construction industry

- Land location, use, urban design and density
- Building adaptability, materials
- Environment, health and well-being
- Social exclusion, community, customer satisfaction, crime and local economy
- Travel, public transport, cycling, pedestrians and cars
- Waste management, pollution (air, noise, vibration)
- Contaminated land
- Landscape, heritage and ecological value, microclimate and open space
- Energy conservation and renewable energy sources
- Water conservation, sewerage and storm water

Source: Crest Nicholson (2002) and Social and Environmental Report, p. 12.

construction industry and also illustrates the link between construction and built environment.

At the same time, it was universally agreed by interviewees and workshop participants that any one player in the construction industry would find it hard to move towards SD because there are many parties responsibility for aspects of the built environment. It was asserted that given no one has overall responsibility for the SD profile of the built environment it is difficult to achieve progress on this front. This complexity has two elements. In a similar way to the oil and gas industry, the users of construction products (householders, for example) will create significant SD impacts regardless of how a building is constructed with those impacts being outside of the control of those who construct the buildings. In the case of the construction industry, however, it was asserted by interviewees that the nature of business processes make diffusion of control over impacts of construction itself even more pronounced. For example, Casella et al. (2002, p. 12) describe the construction life cycle as entailing inception, feasibility, design, procurement, construction and hand-over with earlier stages significantly affect the outcomes of later stages. Further, these various stages involve planners, designers, architects, builders, material manufacturers, landscapers and final users. The diversity of parties involved, along with the interactions between various stages, thus makes construction itself less controllable than (say) oil and gas extraction and refining.

In addition, it was asserted by several of the interviewees that the knowledge base and interest of the ultimate clients and/or users of the built environment with respect to SD are minimal. This observation has two parts. First, the users are themselves diverse (and include all of the UK population living in housing as well and various commercial and non-profit organisations who use buildings) and hence would have a diverse set of requirements for buildings that in turn would reflect different priorities with respect to SD. Second, that within this diverse user group there would be different levels of understanding of SD, with the majority of users having a low level of understanding and little incentive to develop their understanding. This type of observation was made in contrast with the perceived situation in the oil and gas industry that one construction interviewee characterised as having clear industry boundaries, high visibility, clear NGO activity in the sector and generally a lack of trust in their activities. In contrast, these elements were seen to provide a clear impetus within the oil and gas sector for addressing SD via a single strategy. These conditions were not seen to be present in the construction industry. Indeed, Upstream (2003, pp. 29/30) suggested that four key blockages for action on SD for the built environment exist: (1) reiterating interviewees assertions, a lack of effective market demand for sustainable properties (but that demand could be expected to slowly grow); (2) lack of government leadership (by means of legislation, regulation and incentives); (3) a mismatch between costs and benefits of SD (requiring more of a partnership approach and better communication between occupiers and investors/developers and their advisors) and (4) lack of SD literacy within the industry.

All of the above is not to say that there is no progress being made, or that no organisations in the industry are seeking to change their practices. Indeed, a snapshot of what could be possible within the construction industry was drawn from an interview with a construction company that is seeking to embrace the SD agenda. For this organisation three key drivers were described as creating an impetus for addressing SD: (1) their own organisational values (which were noted to have been informed by some adverse experiences with respect to the SD profile of projects in the past); (2) the process of internationalisation (and the fact that this brought to light issues that go to the core of the SD agenda in lesser developed countries) and (3) the nature of their commercial partnerships (in terms of having a significant amount of business and profits tied up in longer-term service contracts with some of these partner organisations having a focus on SD). These drivers have lead this organisation to undertake SD reporting and have also had some impact on internal decision-making processes. In particular, it was noted that the firm had developed SD indicators and had started to develop/experiment with SD plans within business units, scenario planning using SD criteria and using SD aspects in project bidding.

More generally, it was noted that there are any number of measurement systems that could be and are used (and which do operate) to allow an assessment of SD in the context of the construction industry. Perhaps the most well known of these methods is the Building Research Establishment's Environmental Assessment Method (hereafter BREEAM) which is summarised in Table 6.3.

It was evident from the workshop with industry participants that in the area of assessment of SD performance there are many existing tools that could be used to assess SD and that what is needed is not new measurement tools but some way of bringing together a more coherent set of tools that will be used by industry participants.

This view appeared to be widely held and is supported by academic research undertaken under with funding from the EPSRC's (this is one of the UK research funding councils, the Engineering and Physical Sciences Research Council; see http://www.epsrc.ac.uk/

Table 6.3: Summary of BREEAM's rating systems for buildings

BREEAM assesses the performance of buildings in the following areas:

- *Management*: overall management policy, commissioning site management and procedural issues.
- *Energy use*: operational energy and carbon dioxide (CO_2) issues.
- *Health and well-being*: indoor and external issues affecting health and well-being.
- *Pollution*: air and water pollution issues.
- *Transport*: transport-related CO_2 and location-related factors.
- *Land use*: greenfield and brownfield sites.
- *Ecology*: ecological value conservation and enhancement of the site.
- *Materials*: environmental implication of building materials, including life cycle impacts.
- *Water*: consumption and water efficiency.

Source: http://www.breeam.org/.

default.htm for more details) Sustainable Urban Environment Research Programme (see http://www.epsrc.ac.uk/ResearchFunding/ Programmes/InfrastructureAndEnvironment/Initiatives/SUE/default. htm for the full details of this programme and current projects under- way). Researchers have found that in the area of environmental assessment there were a huge array of potential tools with some 25 being assessed in detail from an initial set of 147 possible tools (see Building Research Establishment, 2004, at http://www.sue-mot. org.uk/publications.htm). At the same time, and in the area of sustainability/social tools for assessment, some 100 tools were also reviewed and evaluated (see Levett-Therivel, 2004, at http://www. sue-mot.org.uk/publications.htm). While few of these tools specif- ically addressed all elements of SD, taken together, or in some combi- nation, SD assessment would be greatly advanced by their application. The issue, therefore, appears not to be what tools should be developed but how the take-up of existing tools could be achieved.

In the context of this book, it is worth noting that there is one in-depth case study on SD assessment that conforms more closely to the type of assessment practices that accountants are generally more familiar with. Forum for the Future has undertaken an evaluation of a building project using a form of full cost accounting (see http://www.forumforthefuture.org.uk/finance/finance accounting_page128.aspx for a summary of their work in this area). Their approach is different from the SAM but is broadly similar in its intent and was applied in the building of the Great Western Hospital (this case is also described in Casella et al., 2002). The case study suggests that SD accounting is possible in the construction industry, and that there are clear commercial benefits from applica- tion of such an accounting technique.

In summary, this part of the chapter has sought to demonstrate that for construction (itself an area of considerable importance in terms of SD of an economy) accounting for SD is possible, albeit that currently there are impediments to its implementation. The impediments sug- gested by interviewees and workshop participants in this industry differed from those expressed in the oil and gas sector. In the first instance, the inherent nature of the industry posed problems in terms of 'doing' sustainable construction (even before accounting for this could be tackled). This suggests, importantly, that SD assessment approaches are likely to be different in different industries and that a tool developed in one setting will not necessarily be transferred easily to another setting. One workshop participant stated that types of tools that would be helpful at the current time included those that stimulate the business case for sustainable buildings (such as measuring productivity in buildings or translating measures into the language of risk for those in the design and build side of the industry) as well as tools that helped build partnerships between entities in the industry such that SD could be pursued. In addition, the need to design assessment techniques that 'work' for the numerous small- and medium-sized enterprises (hereafter SMEs) that make up the industry was deemed to be of key importance by two workshop participants. SMEs were perceived to be less interested in SD concepts and also to have less capacity to develop and use tools. In this respect the construction industry differed from the oil and gas sector where the larger industry players have the capacity to develop and experiment with SD evaluation.

Electricity generation

The electricity generation sector is, in some ways, similar to the oil and gas sector and thus was selected as one industry that may be interested in SD assessment. Perceived similarities were that the industry produced a product (energy in the form of electricity), that like fuel energy, was a key component in the current economic system. This industry, however, differs from the oil and gas sector in that there is a greater array of electricity generation technologies available. Technologies include: biomass, coal, gas, hydro, hydrogen, nuclear, oil, solar, tidal and wind, each with their own SD profile. At the same time, debates about externalities of electricity generation are ongoing and heated (for example, over the desirability of nuclear energy as well as the visual impact of wind farms).

While there may be reasons to expect that this industry will be amenable to SD assessment, it proved difficult to locate sector participants who were willing to be interviewed. Many of those who were approached were facing restructuring within their organisations at the time the work was being conducted. It must have also been the case that the project based SD assessment was not high up their priorities. Despite the inability of several companies approached to participate in this work, two interviews were undertaken with industry participants. As a result, all that can be developed here is a very simple picture of SD assessment possibilities in the electricity generation industry.

The political context of electricity generation was identified by interview participants (and indeed was among some of the reasons offered when interviews were declined) as removing the need for entity or project level SD assessment in the electricity generation sector. This context contained several aspects that reduced the probability of SD assessment being pursued. In the first instance quantifying externalities were noted as being very easy for any specific organisation. Given the majority of firms disclosure pollution from generation (stand-alone non-financial reporting is the norm in this industry) the application of some costing factor (for example, that used in the ExternE project: European Commission, 1995) would allow anyone to generate an externalities profile for an organisation (see, for example, Atkinson, 2000, who did just this). Why a firm would seek to promote the use of such figures, however, puzzled one interviewee who noted that given the size of such externalities he did not 'see a huge amount of virtue in publishing this figure'. It seemed to be readily accepted that there are externalities from electricity generation but also that there have been substantial strides made over the last decade to reducing this profile (the Electricity Association, 2002, for example, note that between 1990 and 2000 the UK electricity industry achieved a 23% reduction in its annual emissions of carbon dioxide while simultaneously achieving a 17% increase in electricity consumption. Emissions of sulphur dioxide and oxides of nitrogen likewise reduced substantially (72% and 57% respectively) between 1990 and 1999). Why one would seek to use externalities data in project evaluations, therefore, was not clear to interviewees because it was perceived that there was no way to effectively deal with these externalities from within the organisation. Rather, control over externalities was seen to rest with government/regulators.

It was also noted that the UK (and indeed in North America) electricity markets are highly regulated. As a result, major construction projects for electricity generation are subject to licensing requirements/constraints and the decision to invest in particular generation technologies is not solely under the control of the individual firm. Externalities accounting, therefore, was viewed as possibly being one part of a dialogue with the regulator but being unlikely to inform internal decision-making processes directly. Indeed, one interviewee noted that externalities data is 'meaningless to [company name] … from the point of view of being able to take some action'. Something like the SAM, however, was thought to be potentially useful for the regulator to make sense of the effectiveness of their own policies.

The final aspect that made SD evaluation tools less likely to be used in this industry was the belief that the SD issues of electricity generation were fairly clear. Indeed, one interviewee suggested that (leaving aside nuclear) it is relatively easy to list electricity generation from more to least sustainable in terms of environmental impact (including demand management and energy efficiency initiatives). In terms of the social aspects of SD it was suggested that for electricity this mainly plays out in terms of fuel poverty. As a result, while a SAM type analysis for different technologies would be interesting it would be unlikely to do anything other than confirm expectations. In this respect there was no perception that a SAM would be strategically useful for industry participants.

Conclusions

The aim of this chapter was to briefly explore the extent to which SD evaluation (of the type addressed by the SAM) could be usefully extended to the construction and electricity generation sectors. While there was some interest in the SAM (and tools like it), significant impediments to implementation of SD performance evaluation of this type were uncovered. The impediments, however, were different in each sector and in each instance were related to the interrelationships between industry participants, the regulatory context of the sector and the economic incentives for individual firms. This relatively cursory exploration of the possibilities for SD performance assessment, therefore, suggests that one would have to think carefully about the context within which tools are sought to be applied. This does not mean that the SAM (for example) is not a robust tool but that its application in these sectors would influence behaviour in different ways.

Conclusions

Corporations are undertaking a variety of responses to the SD agenda. Leaving aside responses that focus on subverting that agenda (for example, by lobbying policy makers or appropriating the agenda) many large organisations are seeking to explain to others and themselves how they contribute to the goal of SD. The growth in stand-alone non-financial reporting (variously entitled, environmental, social, corporate citizenship, health, safety and environment, corporate social responsibility, SD and corporate responsibility reporting) from the early 1990s provides evidence of corporate engagement with aspects of the SD agenda. What is hard to infer from stand-alone reporting activities, however, is the extent to which organisations are incorporating SD thinking into their internal decision-making processes. This book sought to explore how SD is and could be incorporated within capital appraisal routines, with a focus on the oil and gas industry.

Specifically, the book introduced in considerable depth one potential evaluation tool, the SAM, as developed and used by BP in an experimental form. The SAM approach fits within the area of evaluation that is most usually described as full cost accounting, which is itself an approach to SD evaluation that monetises impacts from activities and seeks to present externalities data alongside traditional measures of corporate impact. Monetized modelling approaches stand in contrast to other approaches to SD evaluation that focus on presenting indicators of the system under investigation or bringing an array of indicators together using some overall evaluation criteria. Other examples of SD performance evaluation were presented in Chapter 2 of this book so as to provide a context within which the SAM could be understood.

The SAM can be described as a cradle to grave evaluation tool that represents selected economic, resource, environmental and social impacts in monetary terms in the form of a signature graph. While the economic leg of the signature represents money that will eventually flow through the accounts of the organisation, the remainder of the signature represents both positive and negative project externalities.

'Testing' the SAM with a variety of audiences, and examining its application within one organisation, suggests that it is relatively robust in terms of modelling the transformation that arises from a project. Regardless of its descriptive validity, the SAM has been observed to engage individuals' thinking about SD. Having said that, reservations were expressed with respect to how a financially quantified tool can describe fully SD and capture the dynamic of decision making in a complex and uncertain world. For other commentators there is an inherent danger in quantifying SD aspects in money terms as it suggests that all positive and negative impacts can be netted off and as a result everything is tradable once reduced to financial figures. This danger is avoided, to a certain extent, within the SAM by way of applying a decision rule that does not allow capital substitution between different capital categories. In addition, the SAM explicitly allows for the possibility of decision relevant aspects being expressed in non-financial terms and presented along with its financial signature.

The wider potential applicability of an approach, such as that represented in the SAM, was also examined. Here a number of impediments to widespread adoption of SD modelling were encountered. In particular, the 'fit' between an evaluation tool and an organisation's culture, strategy, ethos and existing performance evaluation methods appears to affect the potential for tools to impact on decision making. For some organisations interviewed the SAM did not mesh with their evaluation routines and, therefore, was not seen to be useful. This suggests that the development of generic SD evaluation tools may be an inappropriate goal in the short term (despite the fact that a lack of generic models will hamper benchmarking of performance between organisations).

In addition, in extending the focus from the oil and gas sector to other industries it was observed that SD performance evaluation tools may need to be different from the SAM to adequately capture the SD issues faced by that industry. In particular, the political context, regulatory framework, the structure of an industry and the number of different players in a project life cycle were observed to affect the effectiveness of a performance appraisal approach. This suggests that experimentation that is sympathetic to each industry's circumstances needs to be undertaken, again ahead of any attempt to standardise SD performance assessment.

In summary, for organisations to incorporate the demands of SD into their operations some form of performance assessment is a necessary but not sufficient step to take. This work, in outlining one approach to SD assessment, demonstrates that SD performance assessment is possible, albeit that assessment has not been perfected. Looking forward, a number of critical steps for advancing SD performance assessment can be identified. First, organisations should be encouraged to experiment with and develop their own SD evaluation approaches. This is required if organisations are to develop robust linking of aspirations to operational performance. Second, if such experimentation is being undertaken it would be beneficial for such experiments to be disseminated because there is much that organisations can learn from each other. This book demonstrates that SD performance evaluation, as part of investment decision-making processes, is a potentially powerful way to bring SD considerations into the life of organisations. The way in which this is achieved, however, was dependent on the nature of the organisation involved as well as the industry context for the experiment.

References

AccountAbility (2003). Redefining Materiality: Practice and Public Policy for Effective Corporate Reporting. London: AccountAbility.

Atkinson, G. (2000). Measuring corporate sustainability. Journal of Environmental Planning and Management, 2, 325–352.

Baxter, T., Bebbington, J. and Cutteridge, D. (2004). Sustainability Assessment Model: Modelling economic, resource, environmental and social flows of a project. In The Triple Bottom Line: Does It All Add Up? (Henriques, A. and Richardson, J., eds.), pp. 113–120. London: Earthscan.

Bebbington, J. and Thomson, I. (1996). Business Conceptions of Sustainable Development and the Implications for Accountancy (ACCA Research Report: London).

Bebbington, J. (2001). Sustainable development: A review of the international development, business and accounting literature. Accounting Forum, 25, 128–157.

Bebbington, J. and Gray, R. (2001). An account of sustainability: Failure, success and a reconceptualisation. Critical Perspectives on Accounting, 12, 557–605.

Bebbington, J. and MacGregor, B. (2003). Modelling and Accounting for Sustainable Development. London: RICS Foundation.

Bebbington, J., Gray, R., Hibbitt, C. and Kirk, E. (2001). Full Cost Accounting: An Agenda for Action. London: Association of Chartered Certified Accountants.

Bell, S. and Morse, S. (1999). Sustainability Indicators: Measuring the Immeasurable. London: Earthscan.

Bennett, M. and James, P. (1998a). Environment under the Spotlight – Current Practice and Future Trends in Environment-Related Performance Measurement for Business. London: Association of Chartered Certified Accountants.

Bennett, M. and James, P. (1998b). The Green Bottom Line: Environmental Accounting for Management. Sheffield: Greenleaf.

Bent, D. (2004). Towards a monetised triple bottom line for an alcohol producer. In Sustainability Accounting and Reporting. Environmental Management Accounting Network (EMAN) proceedings.

Building Research Establishment (2004). Assessment of sustainability tools, report for SUE-Mot: Fit for the journey ahead project (see http://www.sue-mot.org.uk/source_files/envtoolevaluation.pdf).

Casella Stanger, Forum for the Future and Carillion (2002). Sustainability Accounting in the Construction Industry. London: CIRIA Publishing Services.

CIRIA (2001). Sustainable Construction: Company Indicators. London: CIRIA.

Cobb, C., Halstead, El, and Rowe, J. (1989). The Genuine Progress Indicator – Summary of Data and Methodology. Washington: Redefining Progress.

Costanza, R. (2000). The dynamics of the ecological footprint project. Ecological Economics, 32, 341–345.

Cox, J., Fell, D. and Thurstain-Goodwin, M. (2002). Red Man, Green Man: Performance Indicators for Urban Sustainability. London: RICS Foundation.

Crest Nicholson (2002). Social and Environmental Report.

Department for Environment, Food and Rural Affairs (2005a). One Future – Different Paths: The UK's Shared Framework for Sustainable Development. London: Department for Environment, Food and Rural Affairs.

Department for Environment, Food and Rural Affairs (2005b). The Validity of Food Miles as an Indicator of Sustainable Development. London: Department for Environment, Food and Rural Affairs.

Department for Environment, Transport and the Regions (1999). A Better Quality of Life: A Strategy for Sustainable Development in the UK. London: Department for Environment, Transport and the Regions.

Department for Environment, Transport and the Regions (2000). Building a Better Quality of Life: A Strategy for More Sustainable Construction. London: Department for Environment, Transport and the Regions.

Department of Trade and Industry (2003). Making the Most of our Built Environment: The Sustainable Construction Task Group. London: Department of Trade and Industry.

Ditz, D., Ranaganathan, J. and Banks, R. D. (1995). Green Ledgers: Case Studies in Corporate Environmental Accounting. Washington: World Resources Institute.

Ekins, P. (2000). Beyond Green GNP: An Overview of Recent Developments in National Environmental Economic Accounting. London: Forum for the Future.

Electricity Association (2002). Electricity and the Environment 2002. London: Electricity Association.

European Commission (1992). Fifth Action Programme: Towards Sustainability, Com (92) 23 final, Vol. I–III. Brussels: European Commission. ISBN 92-77-42828-7. CB-CO-92-151-EN-C.

European Commission (1995). ExternE: Externalities of Energy, Vol. 1–6. Brussels: European Commission.

Gladwin, T. N., Kennelly, J. J. and Krause, T.-S. (1995). Shifting paradigms for sustainable development: Implications for management theory and research. Academy of Management Review, 20, 874–907.

Global Witness (2004). Time for Transparency: Coming Clean on Oil, Mining and Gas Revenues. London: Global Witness.

Gray, R. and Bebbington, J. (2001). Accounting for the Environment (2nd Edition). London: Sage.

Holdgate, M., Kassas, M. and White, G. (1982). The Stockholm Conference. In The World Environment 1972–1982. (Holdgate, M., Kassas, M. and White, G., eds.). London: Tycooly International.

International Union for the Conservation of Nature (IUCN) (1980). World Conservation Strategy. Gland: International Union for the Conservation of Nature – United Nations Environment Programme – World Wildlife Fund.

Jackson, T. and Marks, N. (1994). Measuring Sustainable Economic Welfare: A Pilot Index for the UK 1950–1990. London: Stockholm Environment Institute/New Economics Foundation.

Jacobs, M. (1991). The Green Economy: Environment, Sustainable Development and the Politics of the Future. London: Pluto Press.

Kolk, A. (2005). Environmental reporting by multinationals from the triad: Convergence or divergence? Management International Review, 45, 145–166.

Kolk, A. and Levy, D. (2001). Winds of change: Corporate strategy, climate change and oil multinationals. European Management Journal, 19, 201–509.

Levett-Therivel Consultants (2004). Analysis of sustainability/social tools, report for SUE-Mot: Fit for the journey ahead project (see http://www.sue-mot.org.uk/source_files/socialreportfinal.pdf).

Loh, J. (2000). Living Planet Report 2000. Switzerland: WWF-World Fund for Nature.

McCormick, J. (1986). The origins of the World Conservation Strategy. Environmental Review, 10, 177–187.

McDonald, G. and Patterson, M. (2004). Ecological footprints and interdependencies of New Zealand regions. Ecological Economics, 50, 49–67.

Norgaard, R. B. (1988). Sustainable development: A co-evolutionary view. Futures, 20, 606–620.

Pirages, D. (1994). Sustainability as an evolving process. Futures, 26, 197–205.

Popoff, F. and Buzzelli, D. T. (1993). Full Cost Accounting. Midland: The Dow Chemical Company.

Rawls, J. (1972). A Theory of Justice. Oxford: Oxford University Press.

Redclift, M. (1987). Sustainable Development: Exploring the Contradictions. London: Methuen.

Rees, W. (2000). Eco-footprint analysis: Merits and brickbats. Ecological Economics, 32, 121–130.

Risk and Policy Analysts (2002). Sustainability Report.

Ross, M. (2001). Extractive Sectors and the Poor. Boston: Oxfam America.

Samson, T., Nash, C., Mackie, P., Shires, J. and Watkiss, P. (2001). Surface Transport Costs and Charges: Great Britain 1998. Leeds: Institute for Transport Studies.

Schaltegger, S. (with Muller, K. and Hindrichsen, H.) (1996). Corporate Environmental Accounting. Chichester: Wiley.

Schaltegger, S. and Burritt, R. (2000). Contemporary Environmental Accounting: Issues, Concepts and Practice. Sheffield: Greenleaf.

Scottish Executive (2002). Meeting the Needs: Priorities, Actions and Targets for Sustainable Development in Scotland. Edinburgh: Scottish Executive.

Tisdell, C. (1988). Sustainable development: Differing perspectives of ecologists and economics, and relevance to LDC's. World Development, 16(3), 373–384.

Tisdell, C. (1993). The nature of sustainability and of sustainable development. Environmental Economics, pp. 313–139.

UK Offshore Operators Association Ltd (2001). Striking a Balance: The UK Offshore Oil and Gas Industry Strategy for its Contribution to SD 2001. London: UKOOA.

UK Offshore Operators Association Ltd (2003). Striking a Balance 2003: The Sustainability Strategy Update and Progress Report of the UK Offshore Oil and Gas Industry. London: UKOOA.

UK Offshore Operators Association Ltd (2004). Striking a Balance 2004: The Sustainability Strategy Update and Progress Report of the UK Offshore Oil and Gas Industry. London: UKOOA.

UK Offshore Operators Association Ltd (2005). Striking a Balance 2005: The Sustainability Strategy Update and Progress Report of the UK Offshore Oil and Gas Industry. London: UKOOA.

UK Offshore Operators Association Ltd (2006). Striking a Balance 2006: The Sustainability Strategy Update and Progress Report of the UK Offshore Oil and Gas Industry. London: UKOOA.

United Nations Development Programme (2004). Human Development Report 2004: Cultural Liberty in Today's Diverse World. New York: United Nations Development Programme.

United Nations World Commission on Environment and Development (1987). Our Common Future (The Brundtland Report). Oxford: Oxford University Press.

United States Environmental Protection Agency (1996). Environmental Accounting Case Studies: Full Cost Accounting for Decision Making at Ontario Hydro. Washington: United States Environmental Protection Agency.

Upstream (2003). Sustainability and the Built Environment – An Agenda for Action. London: RICS Foundation.

Wackernagel, M. and Rees, W. (1996). Our Ecological Footprint: Reducing Human Impact on the Earth. Philadelphia: New Society Publishers.

Welsh Assembly Government/Llywadraeth Cynulliad Cymru (2004). The Sustainable Development Action Plan: 2004–2007. Cardiff: Welsh Assembly Government.

World Bank (1995). Mainstreaming the Environment: The World Bank Group and the Environment since the Rio Earth Summit. Washington: The World Bank.

Yanarella, E. J. and Levine, R. S. (1992). Does sustainable development lead to sustainability? Futures, 24, 759–774.

Index

Index

127

Lightning Source UK Ltd.
Milton Keynes UK
29 April 2010

153513UK00001B/18/A